CAMBRIDGE IBERIAN AND
LATIN AMERICAN STUDIES

GENERAL EDITOR
P. E. RUSSELL F.B.A.
Emeritus Professor of Spanish Studies
University of Oxford

ASSOCIATE EDITORS
E. PUPO-WALKER
Director, Center for Latin American and Iberian Studies
Vanderbilt University
A. R. D. PAGDEN
Lecturer in History, University of Cambridge

Christian Martyrs in Muslim Spain

Professor Wolf's book offers important new insights into the so-called 'martyrdom movement' that occurred in Córdoba in the 850s. It includes a biographical treatment of the ninth-century Cordoban priest Eulogius, who witnessed and recorded the martyrdoms of over forty Christians at the hands of Muslim authorities. Eulogius' hagiographical task was complicated by the fact that many of the Christians in Córdoba at the time resented the provocative actions of the martyrs that had led to their executions, claiming that their public denunciations of Islam were inappropriate given the relative tolerance of the emir.

The purpose of this study is threefold: firstly, it analyzes the way in which Eulogius' martyrologies recast both the events and the ideal of sanctity to make the Cordoban martyrs look more like their ancient Roman counterparts. Secondly, it explores the reasons why an important ecclesiastic like Eulogius would want to defend such dubious martyrs in the first place. And thirdly, having come to an understanding about the motives of Eulogius, the study returns to the question of the motives of the martyrs themselves.

This work will be of value to scholars and others with an interest in the history of Muslim Spain, the history of Christian–Muslim interaction, and historical ideas of sanctity.

Christian Martyrs in Muslim Spain

KENNETH BAXTER WOLF

Assistant Professor of History,
Pomona College, Claremont,
California

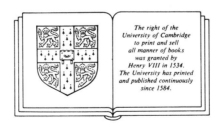

The right of the
University of Cambridge
to print and sell
all manner of books
was granted by
Henry VIII in 1534.
The University has printed
and published continuously
since 1584.

CAMBRIDGE UNIVERSITY PRESS

Cambridge
New York   New Rochelle   Melbourne   Sydney

Published by the Press Syndicate of the University of Cambridge
The Pitt Building, Trumpington Street, Cambridge CB2 1RP
32 East 57th Street, New York, NY 10022, USA
10 Stamford Road, Oakleigh, Melbourne 3166, Australia

© Cambridge University Press 1988

First published 1988

Printed in Great Britain at
the University Press, Cambridge

British Library cataloguing in publication data
Wolf, Kenneth Baxter
Christian martyrs in Muslim Spain. –
(Cambridge Iberian and Latin American
studies. History and social theory).
1. Christian martyrs – Spain –
Córdoba – History
I. Title
272'.9 BR1608.s8

Library of Congress cataloguing in publication data
Wolf, Kenneth Baxter, 1957–
Christian martyrs in Muslim Spain.
(Cambridge Iberian and Latin American studies)
Bibliography.
Includes index.
1. Christian martyrs – Spain – Córdoba (Province)
2. Eulogius, of Córdoba, Saint, ca. 810–859.
3. Córdoba (Spain: Province) – Church history.
I. Title. II. Series.
BX4659.s8w65 1988 272 87-11670

ISBN 0 521 34416 6

SE

To the memory of my father,
Baxter Keyt Wolf,
a different kind of artist

Contents

Acknowledgements

Many individuals contributed to this effort. The subject and method reflect Gavin Langmuir's contagious fascination with questions of religiosity and, more specifically, the process by which one religious community comes to grips with another. Lawrence Berman, Stephen Ferruolo, Sabine MacCormack, and George Brown also offered their insights, as did Martha Newman and William Klingshirn. The encouragement that I received from people like Kent Romanoff and Carlton Tucker made the task much easier.

I would also like to express my gratitude to Robert Burns, S.J., for bringing the manuscript to the attention of Cambridge University Press as well as for his continuous support of the project over the last six years. Raphael Jiménez Pedrajas, too, deserves recognition for his gracious assistance.

My father and mother contributed in an indirect but formative way by fostering the discipline and confidence that would see me through the project. Much more intimate was the involvement of my wife, Mary Kashmar, who saw the work and its author through every one of its ups and downs.

Finally I would like to acknowledge Stanford University and the Whiting Foundation, both of which provided me with the financial support needed to expedite the completion of the manuscript.

Note on transliteration and names

Arabic names and terms have been transliterated consistently with two exceptions: first, words that have entered the English language, such as, emir, caliph, dinar, Allah, mosque, and muezzin; and second, plural forms which, if transliterated accurately, would require confusing orthographic changes. Instead I have simply added an "s" to the singular form, as in the case of *dhimmī*s. I have used al-Andalus interchangeably with Muslim Spain to refer to those parts of the Iberian peninsula under Muslim rule. Readers will find "Andalusian Christians" in place of "Mozarabs" since the former allows for reference to Christians living in Muslim Spain without automatically implying acculturation.

For the sake of consistency, I have rendered all of the names of the martyrs and polemicists in their Latin forms even when there is an English equivalent. Hence "Paulus" instead of Paul and "Joannes" instead of John. Though it may seem awkward, the alternatives are more so. The exceptions are names of figures, such as Augustine or Gregory, whom we know from sources other than the documents pertaining to the martyrdoms. For place names, I have been less consistent. If there is a common English equivalent, I have used it. If not, I use either the Spanish or Latin forms depending on reader accessibility.

Introduction

The city of Córdoba was the setting for an unusual historical drama that unfolded between the years 850 and 859, when forty-eight Christians were decapitated for religious offenses against Islam. More striking than the number of executions were the peculiar circumstances surrounding them. For one thing, as the sources unambiguously demonstrate, the majority of the victims deliberately invoked capital punishment by publicly blaspheming Muḥammad and disparaging Islam. Moreover, though some Cordoban Christians applauded the executed Christians as martyrs, others regarded them as self-immolators whose unwarranted outbursts served only to expose the community as a whole to the emir's suspicions.

Our information about this historical anomaly comes almost entirely from the works of two men who lived in Córdoba during the time of the martyrdoms. Eulogius, a priest, and Paulus Alvarus, an educated layman, reacted to the scorn that the martyrs elicited by composing apologetic treatises on their behalf, extolling their fortitude and defending their memories from the attacks of unsympathetic Christians. Eulogius even went a step further, composing a martyrology through which he transformed the executed Christians into holy martyrs worthy of cultic veneration. His treatises and martyrology, combined with a few letters, make Eulogius the key source of information for what has come to be known as the "Cordoban martyrs' movement."

Previous treatments of the martyrdoms have attempted to lay bare the motives of the participants themselves. Since the martyrs never expressed themselves in writing, such reconstructions have relied almost entirely on Eulogius' depiction of the events, under the assumption that his involvement in the movement was

I

intimate. But to conflate the motives of any hagiographer with those of his protagonists can be very misleading. Writing a book about a saint is not the same as being a saint. In Eulogius' case, though he, too, ultimately suffered the same kind of death, he never in his life actively sought execution in the manner of the martyrs he praised. As useful as Eulogius' works are for recreating the events of the 850s, then, they can really only provide direct information about the thoughts and perceptions of one person: Eulogius.

Our intention is to approach Eulogius' writings more critically and thus more narrowly, using them to answer questions about Eulogius himself. In the first place, we will seek to determine what prompted a priest like Eulogius to lend his literary support to something as unusual and controversial as a series of unprovoked martyrdoms. Rather than assume that he and the martyrs were inspired by the same visions and moved by the same forces, we will be treating Eulogius in isolation, reconstructing his biography and gleaning from it the most likely reasons for his support of the martyrs.

Once we have determined why Eulogius defended the martyrs, we will turn to the question how. For it was clear to everyone, even Eulogius, that the martyrs of Córdoba were not martyrs of the ancient Roman cast. The inconsistencies between the classical paradigm and the circumstances surrounding the executions in ninth-century Córdoba provided the unsympathetic Christians with a way of justifying their opinion of the confessors. In addressing these specific discrepancies, Eulogius not only probed, in an unusually self-conscious manner, the definition of sanctity, but inadvertently provided a window through which we can observe how some Cordoban Christians justified their conciliatory attitudes toward the Muslim authorities.

Using Eulogius' writings to assess his motives and methods not only represents the most reliable use of the sources but it also constitutes the first step toward any accurate understanding of the martyrs. Only when we know who Eulogius was and what he was attempting to do can we begin to extract his influence from his martyrology and proceed, with proper caution, to assess the motives of the Cordoban martyrs themselves.

I
Background

1

Christians in Muslim Córdoba

In late summer of the year 711 a small Muslim contingent under the command of Mughīth ar-Rumī found its way to the bank of the Guadalquivir river opposite Córdoba.[1] There, in a stand of pine trees safely out of sight of the city's sentries, they set up camp and began to reconnoiter the area around the city. Some of the scouts came upon a shepherd, whom they apprehended and brought to Mughīth for questioning. From him the commander learned that the bulk of the Cordoban nobility had already fled north in anticipation of a Muslim assault, leaving the town with a depleted garrison of no more than four or five hundred men. The shepherd also informed him of a large fissure in the otherwise sound and formidable wall that girded the city.

When darkness came it brought with it an unseasonably cold rainstorm which not only helped to obscure the Muslim forces as they crossed the river, but compelled the Cordoban sentries to abandon their posts in search of temporary shelter. With the shepherd as his guide, Mughīth found the aperture and sent a handful of men through it with instructions to open the south gate adjacent to the old Roman bridge. The surprised soldiers fled as the locks on the gate were smashed, allowing the rest of Mughīth's men to ride into the city. Mughīth proceeded to occupy the abandoned palace, enlist the aid of the local Jews to help guard the city,[2] and compose a letter describing his success to his superior, Ṭāriq ibn Ziyād. The only threat to his control of the city was removed some three months later when, after capturing the commander of the Cordoban garrison as he attempted to flee north to Toledo,[3] Mughīth led a successful assault on the soldiers who still held out in the church of St. Acisclus.

The *Akhbār Majmūʿa*, the anonymous source that describes this first encounter between the Muslim conquerors and the peoples of Córdoba, says nothing about Mughīth's subsequent dealings with the vast Christian population that chose not to follow its leaders into exile. We can only surmise, based on the chronicler's silence as well as the general pattern of Muslim conquest, that the Christians who remained offered no resistance. Fortunately the independent account of the historian ar-Rāzī allows us to fill in some of the gaps. In the course of his description of the founding of the famous Cordoban mosque, the chronicler explained that the conquerors appropriated half of the local church dedicated to St. Vincent for use as a mosque. This was not an uncommon stopgap measure for dealing with the religious needs of the victorious armies. Syrians in the town of Hims had experienced similar divisions in the wake of their conquest.[4] But with the steady influx into Córdoba of Arab immigrants over the next two generations, the Muslim worshippers found their quarters increasingly cramped. During the reign of the first ʿUmayyad emir, ʿAbd ar-Raḥmān I (754–88), negotiations began between the emir and the leaders of the Christian community to resolve the problem. Finally, after a promise of a large cash payment as well as permission to rebuild one of the extramural churches that had been leveled at the time of the conquest, the Christians relinquished their half of St. Vincent's. The emir then ordered the demolition of the church to make way for the construction of the mosque that occupies the site to this day.[5]

For our purposes, the most significant fact about this episode is that the Christians specifically appealed to a capitulation agreement, worked out between their grandfathers and the original conquerors of Córdoba, as the legal basis for their claims to the church. Unfortunately the only stipulation of this lost treaty about which we have any direct knowledge is the one to which ar-Rāzī referred: that the Christians would relinquish control over half of the church of St. Vincent's. But by reviewing the capitulation agreements that survive from other parts of the Islamic empire, we can reconstruct the basic components of the original pact offered to the citizens of Córdoba.

Every such agreement reached between Muslim leaders and the peoples they subjected was based in principle on two passages from the Qur'ān:

Fight those who believe not
In God nor the last Day
Nor hold that forbidden
Which hath been forbidden
By God and His Apostle
Nor acknowledge the Religion
Of Truth (even if they are)
Of the People of the Book,
Until they pay the *Jizya*
With willing submission,
And feel themselves subdued.

Those who believe (in the Qur'ān),
And those who follow the Jewish (scriptures),
And the Christians and the Sabians, –
Any who believe in God
And the Last Day,
And work righteousness,
Shall have their reward
With their Lord: on them
Shall be no fear nor shall they grieve.[6]

The militant monotheism that infused the Islamic concept of *jihād* could not tolerate the existence of religious alternatives that recognized neither God's unity nor the inevitability of his judgement. Thus polytheists were given no real choice by their Muslim conquerors but to embrace Islam. The Christians and the Jews were, however, a different matter. Having met the basic monotheistic criterion, their only failure in the eyes of the Muslims was their misinformed, but ultimately tolerable, reluctance to accept Muḥammad as the most recent in the long line of prophetic successors to Abraham. This ambiguity in the religious status of the scriptuaries or "peoples of the book" led to a certain ambiguity in their legal position within Islamic society as well. Though tolerated and protected on the basis of their monotheism, they suffered political subjection and the stigma of a special tax, the *jizya*, as a penalty for their rejection of Muḥammad's prophethood.

The Qur'ān was not the only, or even the most significant, factor influencing Muslim policy toward subject religious communities. The fact that the Muslims were vastly outnumbered by the Christians in the Mediterranean basin limited their options. They could not, even if their scriptures had demanded it, effect a mass conversion of local populations. On the contrary, their early policies suggest that the Muslim rulers and jurists were more concerned about protecting their own people from the potentially polluting effects of close contact with large Christian populations. Limited by their numbers and wary of cultural absorption, the Muslims had every reason to allow a great deal of autonomy to any Christian community that recognized their authority and paid the *jizya*.[7]

The earliest examples of the "covenant of protection" (*dhimma*) which Muḥammad and his generals used to encourage Christian cities to surrender illustrate the confluence of religious, economic, and strategic concerns. In the year 630 the Christians of Ayla received a promise of complete protection of person and property in exchange for the payment of a yearly tribute amounting to one dinar per adult male citizen.[8] In 632 Muḥammad offered the same terms to the Christians of Najran in exchange for their promise to provide clothing and silver in amounts which varied according to the town's yearly production, horses and shields in the event of a local war, and hospitality to any Muslim envoy who might request it.[9]

The treaties offered to the scriptuaries of the cities and territories conquered after the prophet's death reflect his emphasis on tribute in exchange for the protection of traditional liberties. The only such agreement that has survived from the conquest of the Iberian peninsula is no exception. In it, Count Theodemirus of Murcia agreed to recognize the overlordship of ʿAbd al-ʿAzīz and to pay tribute consisting of a yearly cash payment supplemented with specific agricultural products. In exchange, Theodemirus received ʿAbd al-ʿAzīz' promise to respect both his property and his jurisdiction in the province of Murcia.[10]

Even though we lack a copy of the Cordoban *dhimma*, then, we know, on the basis of the pattern established by Muḥammad and followed by his successors, that it must have stipulated the payment of an annual tax, whether in kind or in cash, in exchange for a pledge on the part of the authorities to preserve the personal and proprietary liberties of the *dhimmīs*.[11] Here the certainty ends. Yet on the basis of the special circumstances of the Muslim settlement in Córdoba, we can speculate a bit further about the contents of the lost covenant.

Ar-Rāzī, as we have seen, explicitly recorded that the Muslims appropriated half of the principal Visigothic church for use as a mosque. This, along with Mughīth's occupation of the Cordoban palace, strongly suggests that from the very beginning the Muslims took up residence in the city itself. Though this arrangement may have become the norm in Spain, it contrasted with the settlement patterns in the east, where the Muslim armies preferred to establish garrisons apart from the subdued cities.[12] Such segregation made sense for both strategic and, as we have seen, religious reasons. Later, as Muslim political control grew more secure and the booty and tribute oriented economy gave way to one based more on commerce, the garrison and city began to merge. When this happened the original succinct covenants governing the relations between the *dhimmī* population and the Muslims required significant elaboration in order to salvage some of the social distance that the garrison system had achieved by simple physical segregation. In the generations that followed the early conquests, Muslim rulers promulgated new statutes in an effort to keep the line that separated Muslim and *dhimmī* from being erased.

The fact that Córdoba did not fall to the Muslims until the second decade of the eighth century, a time when Muslim jurists in the east were already implementing such regulations, may explain why its Muslim conquerors did not hesitate to settle within the city itself.[13] The same chronological connection allows us to hypothesize about the types of social limitations under which Christians in Spain lived on the basis of what we know about the better documented legal situation in the eastern Islamic world.

Much of this new legislation aimed at limiting those aspects of the Christian cult which seemed to compromise the dominant position of Islam. ʿUmar II (717–20), whose caliphate produced the first full series of laws designed to keep *dhimmī*s in their place, forbade the construction of any new churches.[14] The so-called pact of ʿUmar I, that came to be considered normative by the legal schools emerging in the eighth century, went even further, forbidding the repair of dilapidated, pre-existing churches.[15] The caliphs and jurists also prohibited rituals and activities that drew too much public attention to Christianity, such as bell ringing or excessively loud chanting in church.[16] Restrictions on processions and funerals were common for the same reasons. The most severe penalties, however, were reserved for those Christians who showed disrespect for Islam: its prophet, its tenets, or its adherents. Any attempt to convert Muslims to Christianity or to prevent Christians who so desired from adopting Islam was considered an act of *lèse majesté*.

Aside from such cultic restrictions most of the laws were simply designed to underscore the position of the *dhimmī*s as second-class citizens. ʿUmar II issued a series of sumptuary laws prohibiting *dhimmī*s from adopting certain characteristically Arab clothing and hair styles.[17] He also seems to have been the first caliph to order all non-Muslim subjects to wear what would later come to be known as the *zunnār*, a distinctive type of belt or girdle, for identification purposes.[18] The pact of ʿUmar also included restrictions on Christian use of arms and saddles as well as characteristically Arabic seals and onomastic structures.[19]

Although from the beginning Christians were given virtual autonomy to govern the affairs of their own religious communities, their subordinate position theoretically restricted their access to government positions which entailed exercise of authority over Muslims. Slaves of Christians could, on the basis of this same principle, win their freedom simply by converting to Islam. Similarly the social position of the *dhimmī* precluded certain types of marital relationships. Sexual relations between a male *dhimmī* and a female Muslim were absolutely forbidden, though a male Muslim could legally marry a Christian or Jew. Muslim jurists may have borrowed this restriction from the Byzantine law books which frowned on the intermarriage of Christians and Jews.[20] Or it may have been a more autochthonous product of the tribal milieu from which Islam emerged. Traditional Bedouin society, which placed great weight on endogamous marriage, considered it a sign of weakness for a clan to lose its female members in marriage to the men of another.[21] If this tribal convention had any impact at all we might expect female members of the Islamic "tribe" (*umma*) to be considered off limits to Christian outsiders.

This proliferation of legal restrictions on Christian activity did not necessarily mean that the actual situation of Christians living under Islam deteriorated to any appreciable degree. For the same inexorable movement toward physical integration that occupied Muslim legal minds inevitably proved stronger than the laws they created. Enforcement always depended on the inclination of the particular authorities involved, and it was typically not in their best interests to carry out the subordination of the *dhimmī* populations to the full extent of the law.

For one thing the Muslims in a given city were almost always outnumbered by the non-Muslim indigenous population, a balance which in many areas was not altered for centuries after the original conquest.[22] In those cities where Christians constituted either the majority or a sizeable minority, the bishops often served in an important ministerial capacity to the local Muslim governors, and not simply in matters pertaining to the Christian community. The late tenth-century bishop Severus of al-Ushmunain in Egypt composed a history of the leaders of the Alexandrian church, which is full of indications of a surprisingly close working relationship between the Egyptian rulers and the patriarchs, who were often used as ambassadors, consulted for political advice, or even solicited for prayer.[23]

The episcopacy was not, however, the only avenue to public service open to Christians. Muslim conquerors often found it to their advantage to leave local administrative structures intact, staffing them with native non-Muslims who were familiar with their workings. The fact that *dhimmīs* lived outside of the intricate network of Arab and Berber tribalism increased their attractiveness to Muslim rulers looking for loyal ministers and public servants who could, if necessary, be easily dislodged. For these reasons, caliphs like ʿUmar II never succeeded in effecting any complete or permanent purge of the bureaucracies of Islam, despite the perennial grumblings of Muslims who resented being placed under the authority of Christians.

While the Arabic sources that pertain specifically to ninth-century Córdoba are largely silent on matters of Christian–Muslim interaction, the Latin documentation provides a good deal of information about such contact and the social liabilities that the Christians of the time faced. On the basis of these sources not only can we reconstruct some of the restrictions on Christian activity that would presumably have been specified in the lost treaty, but we can assess the frequency with which the more universal proscriptions were being enforced.

The Christians of Córdoba were without a doubt subject to

regular taxation. Eulogius complained of a "monthly tribute" that constituted a financial hardship for the Christians.[24] Similarly Alvarus wrote of an "unbearable tax" that weighed heavily on Christian necks.[25] There is little doubt, given the tone of victimization that both men adopted when speaking of the levies and the regularity with which they were collected, that *tributum, vectigal,* and *census* were simply Latin synonyms for the universal *dhimmī* tax, the *jizya.*[26]

The Cordoban authorities also prosecuted Christians guilty of blasphemy. In the spring of 850, a priest named Perfectus was arrested and later executed for publicly expressing his opinions about the errors of Islam to a group of Muslims.[27] Months later a Christian merchant named Joannes suffered a severe lashing, public humiliation, and a long prison term for invoking the prophet's name as he sold his wares in the marketplace.[28] But though diligent in their enforcement of the laws against blasphemy, the emirs of the time were willing to let more venial violations of the ban on public displays of Christianity go unchecked. Bells rang in Córdoba to indicate the canonical hours for the benefit of the faithful.[29] Christian funeral processions passed through Muslim neighborhoods.[30] Interestingly enough, though these acts provoked no official censure, they did at times become a target for public derision. Eulogius complained that the "clang of the reverberating metal" evoked Arabic curses from the Muslims who were within earshot.[31] Alvarus expressed his shock that priests were often subjected to verbal abuse or even pelted with rocks and dung when taking the dead to the cemetery.[32] These popular outbursts, unconnected with any known official action, suggest that laws against bell-ringing and processions had once been promulgated in Córdoba, but had since fallen into desuetude.

The mockery and jeering that some priests suffered as they passed through Muslim quarters in their distinctive clerical garb may also have been a vestige of earlier limitations on the public expression of Christianity.[33] This type of abuse may have been the principal factor in the declining standards of clerical dress decried by Leovigildus, the ninth-century Andalusian author of the *Liber de habitu clericorum.* Leovigildus criticized what he regarded as a "lack of ardor" and a certain "fatuity among some of the clerics," prompted by "Ishmaelite oppression."[34] In the course of the treatise he reviewed the symbolic significance of each aspect of the clerical regalia, apparently for the benefit of those who had reason to question the utility of a uniform that significantly increased their susceptibility to public ridicule. The fact that there are no examples of laymen encountering this type of unprovoked derision strongly suggests that the sumptuary laws which would have served to set every Christian apart were not enforced in ninth-century Córdoba. With the exception of the clergy, Cordoban Christians must have looked much like Cordoban Muslims.[35]

The evidence regarding church fabric in Córdoba also attests to the flexibility of the emirs. As we have seen, Ar-Rāzī explicitly stated that all of the churches except St. Vincent's were torn down in the aftermath of the conquest. As part of the later agreement the authorities permitted the Christians to rebuild one of the extramural churches for their exclusive use. Yet in the course of his writings Eulogius makes mention of no less than thirteen different institutions located in the immediate vicinity of Córdoba: four *basilicae* and nine monasteries, at least two of which were established within the priest's own memory.[36] Half of these monasteries lay in or at the foot of the mountains which border the Guadalquivir valley a few miles north of the city.[37] Most of the others were situated down river.[38] Unfortunately Eulogius was less precise about the exact locations of the churches.[39] But the Arab historian Ibn Haiyan refers specifically to churches both in and outside of Córdoba, suggesting that if indeed the original conquerors did level all the churches except St. Vincent's, subsequent rulers allowed many of them to be rebuilt.[40]

The many examples of Christians in positions of authority within the Cordoban government illustrate the remarkable extent to which the emirs had suspended laws controlling religious integration. ʿAbd ar-Rahmān II worked closely with the bishop Reccafredus to discourage the spontaneous martyrdoms.[41] But bishops were not the only Christians in Córdoba who found themselves in positions of power. The emir al-Ḥakam I (796–822), shaken by a rebellion in a Cordoban suburb in 805, created a special bodyguard headed by the leading secular member of the local Christian community, count Rabiʿ, son of Theodulf.[42] According to other Arabic sources, the same count served as the emir's main tax collector until he was removed and executed for alleged misappropriations.[43] The use of Christians as both soldiers and tax collectors was as commonplace in ninth-century Córdoba as it was throughout the Islamic world, owing, again, to the absence of the tribal loyalties that could potentially compromise the allegiance of an Arab or Berber.[44] Other positions within the Cordoban bureaucracy were equally open to Christians. Samson, who later became an abbot in one of the local monasteries, served on occasion as an official translator to the emir.[45] A Christian nobleman named Argimirus acted in some sort of judicial capacity as Muḥammad I's *censor*.[46] Finally, one of Eulogius' own brothers, Joseph, was a member of the *principatus* in the late 840s, but our source failed to elaborate on the official duties involved.[47]

We also know of two Christians who, perhaps consecutively, occupied the office of *exceptor reipublicae*. Isaac, whom we shall later meet as the first of the spontaneous martyrs, was promoted to the position because of his fluency in Arabic.[48] After he retired from public life the office passed to another Christian, probably the count Ibn Antonian, whom Ibn al-Qūṭīya and al-Khushanī both described as a *kātib*, or secretary, to Muḥammad I.[49] It appears that the office of *exceptor* is identical to what the Arabs referred to as the *kātib adh-dhimam* (secretary of the covenant), whose purpose it was to "attend to the protection and security of the Christians and Jews."[50] The only view that Eulogius provided of the *exceptor* acting in his official capacity had him presiding over the episcopal council in 852 as the direct representative of the emir, a task which would seem to fit the responsibilities of the *kātib adh-dhimam* quite well.[51] It made sense to fill this important position with Arabic-speaking Christians, who could most effectively communicate with the leaders of the largest Andalusian religious contingent.

When all of the evidence from both Latin and Arabic sources has been reviewed, it would appear that for the most part the laws designed to keep Christians and Muslims at what the jurists regarded as the proper social distance went unenforced in ninth-century Córdoba. Taxation and the proscriptions against blasphemy and apostasy are the only apparent exceptions. Of these only the *jizya* could have served as anything like a perennial reminder of the subordinate status of the Cordoban Christians. The occasions for enforcing the other two were, under normal circumstances, simply too few and far between to underscore the religious divisions.

Such was the rather relaxed legal climate that prevailed in Córdoba prior to June 3, 851, when the monk Isaac descended from his mountain retreat and, without provocation, berated a Cordoban judge for failing to recognize the errors of Islam and its prophet. As we shall see in the next chapter, his example led to periodic waves of Christians flouting the proscriptions against blasphemy in their search for a martyr's death. But before we consider their actions in any detail, we must extend our overview of the relationship between the authorities and the Christian community a bit further into the 850s. For with the very first spontaneous martyrs came some significant modifications in the emir's treatment of the Christian population of Córdoba.

When the judge, at whom Isaac had chosen to vent his animosity toward Islam, reported the case to ʿAbd ar-Raḥmān II, the emir ordered the decapitation of the monk and immediately promulgated an edict which reiterated the Islamic prohibition of blasphemy, threatening any subsequent violators with the same punishment.[52] When, over the next four days, seven more Christians followed Isaac's example, the authorities began to worry. Eulogius no doubt exaggerated their reaction when he wrote that "the Muslims were dumbfounded with fear as a result of these events and thought the doom of their republic and the ruin of their kingdom to be at hand."[53] But given the history of local and provincial uprisings against the emirs, it would be a mistake to underestimate their concern over this new form of dissent.

ʿAbd ar-Raḥmān II had experienced more than his share of troubles during the reign of his father. As an adolescent he had witnessed the crucifixion of seventy-two men, from the *rabaḍ shaqunda* on the bank opposite Córdoba proper, who, in 805, had conspired to displace al-Ḥakam with one of his cousins.[54] Thirteen years later, despite the emir's precautions, he came frighteningly close to another violent deposition at the hands of rebels from the same volatile quarter. ʿAbd ar-Raḥmān probably took part in the three day sack and finally the razing of the *rabaḍ* that followed the victory of al-Ḥakam's troops.[55] Though the depopulated right bank would host no more conspiracies, the memories no doubt left the new emir all the more wary of signs of local dissent. Not surprisingly, then, when eight Christians in five days came forward to pronounce judgement on Islam, he reacted swiftly by ordering the arrest and detention of the clerical leadership of the local Christian community.[56]

The imprisonment of the clerics lasted anywhere up to four months, ending in November 851. At first it appeared to have achieved its purpose: the outbursts quickly subsided with only a pair of executions recorded over the next seven months. When, however, the Andalusian summer brought with it a new wave of martyrs, the emir turned again to the Christian leaders as the ones most capable of controlling the zealots. But instead of imprisoning them, he ordered them to convene a council in Córdoba to review the matter and develop some strategy for dealing with the dissidents internally.[57] The result was not exactly what the emir had in mind. The statement which the council drafted, though hardly a vote of confidence for the martyrs, still did not bring any significant ecclesiastical pressure to bear on Christians who might have been considering the same course. The week before ʿAbd ar-Raḥmān's death on September 22, 852, saw the executions of four more Christians.

Muḥammad I, who succeeded his father as emir, followed a different tack in his dealings with the martyrs. He immediately began to apply pressure to the Christian community as a whole by enforcing many of the *dhimma* restrictions that had either never been enforced in Córdoba or had long since been neglected. "On the very day that he received the scepter of the kingdom," wrote Eulogius, "he ordered all Christians to leave the palace, deprived them of their dignity, and removed their honor . . ."[58] This purge led to the expulsion of the incumbent *exceptor reipublicae* who, owing to his exceptional proficiency in Arabic, managed to hang on a few months longer than the rest of the expelled Christians. Ultimately, however, he was reinstated after having, in Eulogius' words, "spurned the holy Trinity and joined the perverse sect."[59]

One interpretation of the motives behind the purge has emphasized the influence of Malikite jurists in the emir's court, whose legal conservatism would not let them stand for breaches of the *dhimma*.[60] Eulogius himself noted that Muḥammad I replaced the Christian officials with Muslims who "laboring with a similar zeal against God, afflicted, subverted and oppressed them everywhere . . ."[61]

And given the strong identification of ninth-century Andalusian jurisprudence with the teachings of Mālik ibn Anas, we would expect Muḥammad I to rely on Malikite ministers to advise him when he came to power.[62] But the same could accurately be said of his father ʿAbd ar-Raḥmān II or his grandfather al-Ḥakam I, both of whom patronized disciples of Mālik, yet apparently did not feel compelled to enforce the *dhimma* restrictions. Furthermore, if the driving force behind Muḥammad's purge was a Malikite-influenced program to put the *dhimmīs* in their proper place, why were the Christians singled out for expulsion? Eulogius himself could not figure it out: "why . . . if the emir enjoyed such free exercise of power, did he not also force the Jews to be removed from his presence . . .?"[63] The answer is simply that the Christians, and not the Jews, were regarded as troublemakers.[64] The hitherto neglected proscriptions against *dhimmīs* were applied specifically to Christians for political reasons, to discourage any further Christian participation in Cordoban dissidence.[65]

Muḥammad was undoubtedly taken aback when, after nine months without a single incident, the Christian Fandila ushered in a new series of martyrdoms with his denunciation of Islam in June 852. The emir responded by reactivating another *dhimma* restriction that, as we have noted, had long since gone unenforced: "He ordered that newly constructed churches be destroyed, as well as anything in the way of refinements that might adorn the old churches, added since the time of the Arab occupation."[66]

Interestingly enough Muḥammad I was unable fully to implement this policy due to military distractions in other parts of al-Andalus. "On all sides the insurgent wars of rebellion brought him great anxiety, for all the cities of Spain, which his father had dominated and occupied with the strength of his forces and the excellence of his power, or had acquired with great remuneration, Muḥammad now bore the responsibility of controlling. When, in various places, he saw his army defeated and put to flight, he lamented, as cities everywhere were diminished and given to ruin."[67] Eulogius, writing sometime in the summer of 853, was not specific about the nature of these *bella dibellionum* that distracted the emir. But fortunately the Arab historians, so attentive to the details of Andalusian military campaigns, recorded the events to which the priest was alluding.

The old Visigothic capital of Toledo, like so many of the other provincial Andalusian centers, perennially resisted the centralizing efforts of the emirs of Córdoba.[68] In Toledo's case much of its recalcitrance stemmed from the fact that neither the Arabs nor the Berbers had ever settled the city in any great numbers, leaving it in the hands of an indigenous population, which, by the mid-ninth century, was composed primarily of Christians and converts to Islam, or *muwallads*.[69] Upon the death of ʿAbd ar-Raḥmān II in September of 852, the two Toledan factions joined in revolt against Córdoba and occupied the nearby town of Calatrava. During the following summer a Cordoban army under the direction of the new emir's brother managed to retake Calatrava and establish a permanent garrison there. But undaunted, the Toledan forces wreaked havoc in the Andújar area, where they ambushed a Cordoban battalion and set ablaze the farmlands of the Jandula valley. Meanwhile the Toledan leaders were cementing an alliance with the new Asturian king, Ordoño I, who, like many Spanish Christian kings before and after, was more than willing to take advantage of internal strife in al-Andalus to extend his own political power. In June of 854, at the Guadacelete creek just southeast of Toledo, the forces representing the Asturian–Toledan alliance met the Cordoban army, led by Muḥammad himself, and were soundly defeated.[70] But in spite of the victory the emir was still unable to force Toledo into submission. Like Tudela, Zaragoza and Huesca which were at that time ruled independently by the powerful *muwallad* clan of the Banū Qasī, and Mérida then under the control of the Berber Banū Tajit, Toledo remained stubbornly outside of Muḥammad's sphere of influence.[71]

It is interesting that Eulogius regarded these "wars of rebellion" that "brought great anxiety" to Muḥammad I as a windfall which saved the bulk of the Cordoban churches from ruin. For in fact it would appear that the rebellion in Toledo was the main reason why the new emir applied such pressure on the Cordoban Christian community when the martyrdoms resumed in June 853.[72] The Toledan uprising, timed to correspond with an expected period of political weakness under a new emir, not only posed a dangerous challenge to Muḥammad's authority, but, because it involved Toledan Christians attempting to forge an alliance with the Christian kingdom of Asturias, must have worn thin any restraint that he might otherwise have exercised toward dissident Christians in his own capital. The purge of Christian officials that Muḥammad had effected in September 852, had not, as it turned out, stifled the suicidal outbursts against Islam. Clearly the emir's plan to destroy churches was conceived with the same goal in mind: to pressure the Christian community as a whole into controlling its more radical exponents at a time of particular political stress.

That Muḥammad regarded the Cordoban dissidents in much the same way as he regarded the rebels that threatened his control of the provinces is apparent from Eulogius' account of another of his abortive plans for dealing with the martyrs. In the wake of the new outbreak in the summer of 853, Muḥammad toyed with the idea of "killing all Christian men and dispersing their women by selling them into slavery, except those who spurned their religion and converted to his cult."[73] His ministers, however, advised him against such an extreme measure. They pointed out that "no wise or urbane Christian, nor any of their leaders, had perpetrated these actions and on that basis asserted that Christians as a whole ought not to perish." The reasoning of the advisors suggests that they were contrasting the unorganized, apolitical disturbances in Córdoba, with the full-fledged rebellions of the north for the benefit of an emir who tended to conflate the two into a single challenge to his authority.

Combining the evidence from ninth-century Latin sources with the information we can glean from earlier Arabic sources from the eastern part of the Islamic empire, we have come to some important conclusions about the relationship between the Andalusian emirs and their Christian subjects. Ar-Rāzī's account of the negotiations leading up to the construction of the Cordoban mosque attests to the existence of a *dhimma* regulating Christian activities and their relations with Muslims. Similar agreements between Muslim leaders and their *dhimmī* subjects in the east allowed us to speculate as to the contents of the lost Cordoban pact. Though we suspect that the Cordoban law books contained all the usual restrictions on Christian activity, there is little evidence to suggest that the ʿUmayyad emirs were ever diligent about enforcing them. In fact the Latin sources dating from the 850s and 860s lead to the exact opposite conclusion. Aside from the *jizya*, the liabilities of Christian life in al-Andalus were minimal. Of all the traditional legal restrictions placed on the exercise of Christianity, the only ones for which we have any evidence of consistent enforcement are the proscriptions against blasphemy and apostasy.

But just because the laws were not being enforced does not mean that they could not be enforced at the discretion of the ruler. Just as it was in the emir's interest during times of peace and prosperity to elevate Christians to positions of public service, to permit them to build churches, and in general to allow them to assimilate into Cordoban society, so in times of stress did it make sense to restore the social barriers and the sense of Christian subordination by enforcing the traditional restrictions. The relations between the emirs ʿAbd ar-Raḥmān II and Muḥammad I and the Christian community of Córdoba in the early 850s should be seen in terms of one of these shifts in policy, one which was elicited by a coincidental series of provincial rebellions and local martyrdoms.

11
The martyrs

2

The martyrs of Córdoba

Who were the martyrs who contributed so much to the anxiety of the emirs? What prompted their suicidal outbursts against Islam? The limitations of the sources make these questions difficult to answer. The only martyr who left any written record was Eulogius and, as we shall see in a subsequent chapter, there is every reason to believe that he was not representative of the group as a whole. For the most part, what we know about the other martyrs is what Eulogius chose to report about them. Though it can be risky to rely on a martyrology which, true to its genre, inflates its protagonists to heroic proportions, we can trust Eulogius at least to identify the martyrs and to inform us of the circumstances surrounding their deaths.

Isaac was the first and probably most politically prominent of the martyrs.[1] His noble birth and training in Arabic contributed to his rise within the local government to one of the highest positions to which a non-Muslim could aspire: that of *kātib adh-dhimam* (secretary of the covenant), or, as Euloguis called it, *exceptor rei-publicae*. Sometime later, he relinquished his post and retired to the monastery at Tabanos, located in the mountains just north of Córdoba.

Isaac remained at Tabanos for three years. Then one day he left his retreat and returned to Córdoba. Approaching the emir's palace where he had once been employed, he asked the *qāḍī* (judge) for some instruction in the fine points of Islam.[2] No sooner had the official begun to elaborate on the life of Muḥammad when the monk burst out with a vituperative attack against Islam, claiming that its "prophet" was languishing in hell for having misled the Arabs.

The *qāḍī* was dumbfounded. His first reaction was to slap Isaac,

but he restrained himself when his counsellors reminded him that
Islamic law protected the accused from physical harm prior to
sentencing. At the suggestion that he must either be drunk or mad
to disparage Islam in the presence of a *qāḍī*, Isaac assured him that
the "zeal of righteousness" compelled him to speak out against
Islam and that he was prepared to die for his indiscretion.[3]

After arresting Isaac and reporting the case to ʿAbd ar-Raḥmān
II, the *qāḍī* sentenced the monk. On June 3, 851 he was decapitated
and suspended upside down for public viewing on the opposite
bank of the river.[4] His body was then cremated and its ashes cast
into the Guadalquivir.[5]

The response of the Muslim judge to Isaac's outburst is
significant. Not only was he, in Eulogius' words, *stupore nimio
turbatus*, but he felt compelled to consult the emir before acting in
his judicial capacity. Isaac's case was apparently unusual. But it is
important to realize that neither the crime nor the punishment
themselves were new. Less than fifteen months before, the authorities had also condemned the priest Perfectus for blasphemy. As we
shall see, however, the circumstances were significantly different.

Perfectus, who served at the basilica of St. Acisclus just outside
the city walls, was stopped one day on his way to market by a group
of Muslims.[6] Seeing that he was a priest, they asked him to explain
the "catholic faith" and to share with them his opinions about
Christ and Muḥammad. Fearing that he would only provoke his
audience, Perfectus declined. But when the Muslims swore to
protect him, he proceeded, in Arabic, to decry Muḥammad as one
of the false prophets foretold by Christ and as a moral reprobate
who had seduced the wife of his kinsman.[7]

Though angered by the harsh attack, the Muslims respected
their oaths and let Perfectus go on his way. But a few days later the
priest ran into some of the same group, who no longer felt
constrained by their earlier promise. Seizing Perfectus, they took
him before the magistrate and testified that he had disparaged the
prophet. As they led Perfectus to prison to wait out the holy month
of Ramaḍān, he repeatedly denied his guilt. Only when he realized
that his fate was sealed did he repeat his denunciation of Islam. On
April 18, 850, Perfectus was decapitated before the crowds that had
gathered to celebrate the end of the feast.[8]

The novelty of Isaac's case, then, was not that he blasphemed

Muḥammad or that he was sentenced to death for it. What was new was the manner in which he broke the law. His actions were deliberate and provocative, specifically designed to bring about his own death. This willful disobedience was precisely what concerned the authorities, prompting them to consider drastic measures to forestall future outbursts.

ʿAbd ar-Raḥmān II's edict, threatening any future blasphemers with execution, was not a well-conceived deterrent for those Christians attracted by Isaac's example. Just two days after the monk's death, a young Christian soldier named Sanctius was decapitated for the same crime. Born in Albi in southern France, Sanctius was captured as a boy and raised to serve in the Cordoban army, perhaps in the palace guard established by the emir's father. It is not clear, from the unusually brief *passio* that Eulogius composed for Sanctius, whether or not Isaac's example was the principal motivating factor behind the martyrdom.[9]

More explicit are the connections between Isaac and the six Christians who died within yet another forty-eight hours. Petrus, a priest from Ecija, thirty miles southwest of Córdoba, and the deacon Walabonsus from Elche on the southeast coast of Spain, had come to Córdoba to study.[10] At the time of their deaths, they were serving as the supervisors of a convent dedicated to Mary just west of Córdoba in the village of Cuteclara. Sabinianus from Fronianus, a small mountain village twelve miles northwest of the city, and Wistremundus, another native of Ecija, had recently entered the monastery of St. Zoylus, some thirty miles north of Córdoba. Joining these four were Habentius, a native Cordoban residing at St. Christopher's just down river from Córdoba, and Hieremia, a kinsman of Isaac and a founder of the monastery at Tabanos. All six presented themselves together before the authorities and made their intentions and inspiration very clear: "We abide by the same confession, O judge, that our most holy brothers Isaac and Sanctius professed. Now hand down the sentence, multiply your cruelty, be kindled with complete fury in vengeance for your prophet. We profess Christ to be truly God and your prophet to be a precursor of antichrist and an author of profane doctrine." Their executions brought the total number to eight in less than a week.[11]

A month later three more Christians set out on the increasingly well-worn path to martyrdom. The deacon Sisenandus had, like Petrus and Walabonsus, come to Córdoba to study, in his case from Beja, in the southwest corner of the peninsula. Inspired by their example and by a vision in which the two martyrs beckoned him to join them, he died on July 16. Sisenandus' example in turn prompted a deacon named Paulus, from the church of St. Zoylus, to sacrifice himself four days later. Within a week a monk from Carmona named Theodemirus added his name to the growing list of martyrs.[12]

After the death of Theodemirus on July 25, 851, the executions subsided for three months. The next victims were Flora and Maria, the first of nine females whose names appear in Eulogius' martyrology. Maria's father, a Christian landowner, had married a Muslim woman whom he had subsequently converted to his own religion. Forced, as a consequence of her marriage and apostasy, to leave their family lands in Elche, the couple came with their two children to live in the village of Fronianus. Shortly afterwards Maria's mother died and her father decided to adopt a penitential lifestyle. So he arranged for his son, Walabonsus, to pursue studies at the local monastery of St. Felix and his daughter to go to the convent in Cuteclara. The two siblings were later reunited when Walabonsus was appointed to act as one of the convent's supervisors.

The death of her brother in June had a profound effect on Maria. This, combined with the fact that her abbess, Artemia, had witnessed the execution of two of her sons thirty years before, no doubt contributed to her decision to follow in her brother's footsteps.[13] While praying for guidance at the church of St. Acisclus, Maria met Flora.[14]

Flora was also the product of a religiously mixed marriage. Her mother, a Christian from the village of Ausianos just west of Córdoba, had married a Sevillan Muslim who died while Flora was still quite young. Deprived of this paternal influence, the girl grew up as a Christian. Well aware that children of mixed marriages legally had no choice but to be Muslim, the mother and daughter worked together to keep Flora's Christianity a secret from her older Muslim brother. Ultimately the tension forced her to run away from home in the company of a sympathetic sister.[15] Her hopes of practicing her religion in peace were spoiled, however, when her brother, apparently an influential figure in Córdoba, began to put pressure on the Christian community, forcing Flora to return. When neither threats nor promises had any effect on her resolve to remain Christian, he turned her over to the authorities. Despite Flora's defense that she had been a Christian from birth and was therefore innocent of the charges of apostasy, Flora was sentenced to a severe whipping and placed on probation in her brother's custody. No sooner had her wounds healed, however, than she fled again, this time taking refuge at a Christian household before leaving town with her sister. Ultimately, however, she decided to return and suffer the consequences.[16]

It is important to realize that though Flora and Maria approached the *qāḍī* and denounced Islam together, they were, in fact, guilty of two distinct crimes. Flora, as the daughter of a Muslim, was legally an apostate. Unlike her predecessors, she was a fugitive long before she presented herself before the magistrate. Her subsequent treatment by the authorities reflected the special nature of her offense. In contrast to the blasphemers, whose fates were sealed from the moment they opened their mouths, she was given ample opportunity in prison to avert her sentence by renouncing Christianity and assuming her proper religious identity.[17]

Aside from Flora and Maria, only two other Christians died in Córdoba between July 851 and July 852. Gusemindus had come from Toledo with his parents, who had dedicated him to the priesthood and arranged for his training at the basilica of St. Faustus, St. Januarius, and St. Martialis. On January 13, 852, he and the monk Servus Dei, who was associated with the same institution, delivered their confessions before the authorities and were put to death.[18]

The six-month lull that followed the executions of Gusemindus and Servus Dei ended in July with the deaths of five more Christians: Aurelius, Sabigotho, Felix, Liliosa, and Georgius. Aurelius' father was, like Flora's, a Muslim who had married a Christian. Apparently orphaned at an early age, the boy was raised by a paternal aunt, who directed his studies toward Arabic literature. But again like Flora, Aurelius harbored a secret longing for Christianity and began to seek out priests for his instruction. When he had come of age, his relatives selected what they thought to be a suitable spouse, not knowing that the young woman,

Sabigotho, was also a secret Christian. In her case, both of her parents had been Muslims, but when her widowed mother remarried, she happened to pick a clandestine Christian who succeeded in converting his new wife. At the time of Sabigotho's marriage to Aurelius, she had long since embraced the religion of her stepfather.

Aurelius had a relative named Felix who, to make things even more complicated, had been born of Christian parents and converted to Islam, only to decide that he had made a mistake. This also constituted apostasy, so he too had to practice his Christianity in private. But he managed to find a sympathetic mate in Liliosa, who, like Sabigotho, was a *filia occultorum Christianorum*.[19]

The two couples concealed their Christianity for some years, and perhaps would have continued to do so, had not Aurelius witnessed the whipping and humiliation of the Christian merchant Joannes, who, as we saw in the first chapter, had indiscreetly sworn by the name of Muḥammad.[20] Struck either by the injustice of the punishment or the fortitude of the victim, Aurelius decided that it was time to make public his Christianity regardless of the consequences. Together with Sabigotho, he adopted a severe penitential program in preparation for martyrdom. For one thing they transformed their marital relationship into a fraternal one so as to generate "spiritual offspring" to match the two children they had produced in their previous life. They also began frequenting the Cordoban prison where they visited not only Joannes, but sought advice from the imprisoned Eulogius.[21] More significantly, Sabigotho met Flora and Maria. In fact, she "frequently visited their cell . . . and stayed at night as if she herself were shackled, not only to console the two soldiers, but to confide in them her own intention to die."[22] Her devotion to the confessors paid off. During the vigil that Sabigotho kept after the execution of Flora and Maria, the two virgins appeared to her in all their newly-won, martyrial glory, and promised that she would ultimately join them. Sabigotho's time, they said, would be at hand when a foreign monk arrived to share her fate.

With renewed vigor, Sabigotho and Aurelius readied themselves for what they now felt certain was their destiny. They sold all their worldly possessions and spent their last days at Tabanos, where they not only prepared for their deaths but arranged for the care of their children. Finally the promised sign appeared in the form of a monk from Palestine named Georgius.

Born in Bethlehem, Georgius resided in the large monastery of St. Sabba just south of Jerusalem. There he not only learned Greek, Latin, and Arabic but engaged in certain austerities, which would win for him the unbounded admiration of, among others, Eulogius, who was particularly impressed that Georgius had never taken a bath.[23] The chain of events leading up to his arrival in Córdoba began when his abbot sent him on a mission to solicit donations from daughter monasteries in North Africa. There Georgius found the church so "oppressed by the incursion of tyrants" that he decided to take a detour to Spain. Again he was surprised by the affliction he found. Leaving the city of Córdoba, he proceeded north to Tabanos, where the abbess Elizabeth, apparently recognizing him as a portent, referred him to Sabigotho. A dream identified him as the one for whom she had been waiting, and henceforth the monk and the couple sought martyrdom together. Soon Felix and Liliosa, having sold all of their porperty, joined them as well.

When the day of their public profession arrived, the women entered a church with unveiled faces and were immediately detected and arrested as apostate Muslims.[24] Meanwhile Aurelius, after making the final arrangements for his children, waited at home with Felix in anticipation of his own arrest. The soldiers came shortly after and marched them all to the judge. At first, the guards ignored Georgius. Their task had been to arrest the husbands of the apostates. But Georgius' quick verbal assault on Islam sufficed to bind his fate with that of the others.

As in the case of Flora, the newly discovered apostates were granted every opportunity to change their minds, but remained unmoved: "Any cult which denies the divinity of Christ, does not profess the essence of the Holy Trinity, refutes baptism, defames Christians and derogates the priesthood, we consider to be damned." After a four day imprisonment, the captives still refused to relent. The authorities, who had not heard Georgius' earlier diatribe, gave him permission to leave. The monk responded with a new outburst for their benefit, and, on July 27, 852, five more Christians were put to death.[25]

During that same summer, six more joined the ranks of martyrs.

Christophorus was a Cordoban-born monk residing at the monastery of St. Martin at Rojana in the mountains above the city. Learning of the other martyrs, he came forward to offer his confession and was immediately imprisoned pending execution. There he met Leovigildus, a monk from Granada who lived in the mountain monastery of St. Justus and St. Pastor, some fifteen miles north of Córdoba. He too had denounced Islam and on August 19 was killed along with Christophorus.[26]

The week prior to ꜥAbd ar-Raḥmān's death on September 22, 852, brought with it four more cases of blasphemy. Emila and Hieremias, childhood companions who had been educated together at the church of St. Cyprian, delivered an especially forceful denunciation of Islam in Arabic, one which served only to multiply the frustration of the dying emir.[27] As if to add insult to injury, the monk Rogelius from a village near Granada and the Syrian pilgrim Servus Dei entered the Cordoban mosque and, to the horror of the Muslim worshippers present, preached the truth of the gospel and the falsehood of Islam. Saved by the authorities from death at the hands of the irate crowd, the two were sentenced to a particularly grisly punishment for desecrating the mosque: their hands and feet were amputated prior to their decapitation.[28]

As we have already seen, one of the first official actions of the new emir, Muḥammad I, was to purge the Cordoban bureaucracy of Christians. He must have been pleased with the apparent effect of this change in policy: the next nine months passed without incident. But again, as summer approached, a new parade of martyrs stepped forth.

Fandila, from the town of Guadix just east of Granada, had, like so many of the other martyrs, come to Córdoba *gratia discendi*. Residing first at Tabanos under abbot Martinus, Fandila rose to the priesthood, serving the needs of the monks of the nearby monastery at Pinna Mellaria. It was Fandila's vituperative confession which, according to Eulogius, pushed the emir to the point of considering the most drastic of measures for silencing the Cordoban Christians. He settled, however, for Fandila's head on June 13, 853.[29]

The very next day, three more Christians died. The priest Anastasius, who received his training at the church of St. Acisclus, turned to the monastic life before finally "descending to the forum" to offer his confession. He was joined by the monk Felix, a native of Alcalá de Henares, fifty miles northeast of Toledo. Though of Numidian Muslim parentage, Felix was exposed to Christianity in Asturias, and later converted. The nun Digna from Tabanos, inspired by a vision of St. Agatha and by the news of the double execution, added her own name to the martyrology before the sun had set. The following day, an aged laywoman named Benildus sacrificed her life as well.[30]

The fact that two of the first five Christians executed under the new emir had been associated with the monastery of Tabanos, an institution that had already produced more than its share of martyrs, must have simplified Muḥammad's decision about where to begin enforcing the restrictions on church building.[31] But the legacy of Tabanos as a fertile breeding ground for confessors outlived the monastery, which was leveled in the summer of 853. Columba, the sixth Christian to die under Muḥammad I, was the sister of Elizabeth and Martinus, two of the co-founders of Tabanos. Having fortuitously evaded her mother's plan to give her away in marriage, Columba followed her siblings into their cloister. When the Muslims arrived to close Tabanos, she took up residence at the basilica of St. Cyprian, where she prepared herself penitentially for a martyr's death. On September 17 she was decapitated.[32]

Columba's example in turn prompted the nun Pomposa to seek martyrdom. Her parents had founded the monastery of St. Salvador at Pinna Mellaria which had already contributed the martyr Fandila. Now, three months later, Pomposa prepared to follow his example. Despite the efforts of her fellow nuns to dissuade her, she escaped to Córdoba, where she died on September 19, 853.[33]

After Pomposa's death, the executions became increasingly sporadic. Abundius, a priest from Ananellos in the Sierra Morena, died ten months later (July 11, 854) as the result of what Eulogius referred to as the "trickery of the gentiles."[34] Perhaps, like Perfectus, he unwittingly blasphemed Muḥammad. In any case, another ten months would pass before the next executions. The priest Amator, who had come to Córdoba from a village near Jaén to study, joined forces with the monk Petrus from Pomposa's monastery of Pinna Mellaria, and Ludovicus, a brother of the deacon Paulus who had been one of the earliest martyrs in the summer of 851. All three were executed for blasphemy on the last day of April 855.[35] At some unspecified point during the same year another Christian was executed for apostasy. This was the layman Witesindus from Cabra, thirty miles southeast of Córdoba, "who suffered a lapse of the holy faith" and converted to Islam only to convert back again.[36]

Helias, a priest from western Spain, and two monks named Paulus and Isidorus blasphemed and died on April 17, 856.[37] Two months later, Argimirus, a nobleman from Cabra who served as Muhammad I's *censor*, was executed for the same crime, but under very different circumstances.[38] Having, like Isaac, "retired from the administration of justice to inhabit the peace and quiet of a monastery," he was accused by Muslims of having degraded the prophet and professed the divinity of Christ. The emir gave him a rare chance to save his life by embracing Islam, but Argimirus refused and was hung up alive on a gibbet before being killed on June 28, 856.[39]

Three weeks later the virgin Aurea was executed, again under quite unique circumstances. Her father had been a Sevillan Muslim, yet for more than thirty years she lived with her mother Artemia as a nun in the convent at Cuteclara without the knowledge of her Muslim relatives. During that time she had seen her two brothers Joannes and Adulphus executed for apostasy in the early 820s, and witnessed the deaths of Petrus, Walabonsus, and Maria, who were associated with her convent in the early 850s. When some of her Muslim relatives came from Seville and recognized her, they brought Aurea to a judge for religious rectification. Offered the choice of renouncing her Christianity or suffering the penalty for apostasy, Aurea opted for the former and was released. But bothered by her lack of fortitude she continued to practice Christianity, all the time preparing herself for her second encounter with the authorities. Finally discovered by her family to have relapsed, she was imprisoned and executed.[40]

The final two martyrs whose passions Eulogius recorded were Rudericus and Salomon. The former was a priest in Cabra whose family life was complicated by the fact that one of his two brothers had converted to Islam. Once, while Rudericus was intervening to break up a fight between his brothers, he received a blow which left him unconscious. His Muslim brother then dragged him through the streets claiming that Rudericus had decided to embrace Islam. Upon regaining his senses and realizing what had happened, he left town fearing that he might be arrested for apostasy. He found what appeared to be a safe hideaway in the mountains above Córdoba, but one day he ran into his Muslim brother. Finding himself in front of the local *qāḍī*, Rudericus denied the charge of apostasy on the grounds that he had never abandoned his Christianity in the first place. But his plea of innocence fell on deaf ears. The judge offered him the standard apostate's choice: accept Islam or die.[41] In prison Rudericus met Salomon, a Christian layman from some unspecified foreign land, who, like Felix and Witesindus, had converted to Islam and then reconverted to Christianity. After three attempts to change their minds, the authorities ordered them executed on March 13, 857.[42]

This is where Eulogius' martyrological accounts end. Yet we know that the executions did not cease with the deaths of Rudericus and Salomon in 857. Alvarus informs us that two years later the authorities arrested the virgin Leocritia for apostasy. "Begotten from the dregs of the gentiles," Leocritia was introduced to the teachings of Christianity by a relative named Litiosa. At first no one suspected that Leocritia's frequent visits to Litiosa's home were anything more than social. Even after her parents discovered the truth and tried to dissuade her, Leocritia refused to relent. But like Flora, Leocritia began to fear the spiritual consequences of practicing her religion surreptitiously. Using messengers, she sought the advice of Eulogius and his sister Anulo, who, like Litiosa, was also a "virgin dedicated to God." Both encouraged her to leave home. So as to be able to depart without arousing suspicion, Leocritia made it appear as if she were attending a wedding. But no sooner was she out of sight than she hastened to meet Eulogius and Anulo. Like Flora's brother, Leocritia's parents responded by applying pressure on the Christian community in an attempt to determine her whereabouts. But in this case the search efforts were hindered by Eulogius who made certain that the girl never stayed in any one hiding place for very long. Eulogius continued to meet with Leocritia to instruct her in the finer points of the faith. But after one of these sessions, her appointed escort failed to appear to lead her to her latest hiding place. A tip led the authorities to the house, where they not only arrested Leocritia for apostasy, but

Eulogius for proselytizing. On March 11, 859, Eulogius was decapitated.[43] Three days later Leocritia met the same fate.

Within the next year, two more Christians were executed. An envoy sent by Charles the Bald to gather information about the martyrs Aurelius and George, whose bodies had been recently translated to Paris, returned to report that he had witnessed the execution of the two sisters while he was in Córdoba.[44] Shortly afterward, according to abbot Samson, "a certain Christian was punished for blaspheming the one whom the *gens Caldea* venerate as a prophet."[45]

Though we have no evidence of any more executions for the duration of the ninth century, a variety of sources, even some Arabic ones, refer to similar incidents in the first half of the tenth. Sometime during the latter part of ʿAbd Allāh's emirate (888–912), a Christian woman named Dhabba came before the Cordoban *qāḍī* claiming that Jesus was God and that Muḥammad had lied to his followers.[46] A few years after her execution, the *qāḍī* Aslam ibn ʿAbd al-ʿAzīz (913–920) was confronted with a Christian "requesting his own death." The judge's biographer wrote, by way of explanation, that "the nonsense or ignorance of the Christians led them to attribute great merit to this action of offering themselves to death."[47] An inscribed piece of marble, uncovered in the sixteenth century in Córdoba, allows us to identify still another martyr, Eugenia, who died on March 26, 923, but the circumstances of her death are unknown.[48]

In contrast to the lack of detail about these three martyrs, the accounts of Pelagius and Argentea, who died in 925 and 931 respectively, are full of information. Pelagius was ten years old when his father, a Galician nobleman, sent him to ʿAbd ar-Raḥmān III's court in Córdoba as a hostage in return for the release of the boy's uncle, Bishop Hermogius of Tuy, who had been captured during a recent skirmish between Christian and Muslim forces. The boy remained confined for three and a half years until, according to the author of the *passio*, the caliph summoned him, offering him a life of ease in exchange for his conversion to Islam and his submission to the caliph's sexual advances. Pelagius refused both requests and was tortured and killed on June 26, 925.[49]

Argentea, the daughter of the great Andalusian rebel leader ʿUmar ibn Ḥafṣūn (d. 917), converted to Christianity and entered a monastery in the vicinity of Córdoba. There she met Vulfura who, according to the anonymous *passio*, had come to Córdoba from France in response to a vision that had revealed to him his martyrial destiny. The authorities imprisoned Vulfura after they discovered him publicly preaching the gospel, and later arrested Argentea who, on one of her visits to the prison, was recognized as the daughter of ʿUmar ibn Ḥafṣūn. The authorities gave both of them the chance to convert to Islam and avoid execution, but they refused and were killed on May 13, 931.[50]

There is no reason to suppose that the martyrdoms ceased in 931 or, for that matter, that we even know about all of the incidents that occurred in the eighty or so years covered by the extant documentation. Eulogius' martyrology would seem to have exhausted the cases from 851 to 859, but after his death we know of no one who shared his interest in maintaining a catalogue of executed Christians. In other words, what might seem at first glance to be a significant decrease in the incidence of executions after 859 may have as much to do with the death of a hagiographer as with any real decline in the number of victims. Because we know of cases after Eulogius' time that were never incorporated into any martyrology we have to assume that, as unprecedented as the high incidence of spontaneous martyrdom in the early 850s was, the decision on the part of a Cordoban priest to record the victims' passions was equally unusual. Before we try to understand what prompted Isaac and the rest to provoke the authorities, we need to determine what motivated Eulogius to compose the *passiones* and promote their cults. As we shall see in the next chapter, this is not a part of the episode that has received its proper share of scholarly attention.

3

The martyrs of Córdoba and their historians

The abundant attention that the martyrs of Córdoba have
attracted in the last four hundred years stands in marked contrast
to the relative neglect they suffered in the first seven centuries after
their deaths.[1] The only manuscript of Eulogius' writings known to
have survived to modern times was one which presumably
accompanied his own remains to Oviedo, where he was translated
in 884. There it lay until the sixteenth-century bishop and in-
quisitor general Pedro Ponce de León happened to fall upon it in his
search for collections of saints' lives.[2] In 1571 the bishop forwarded
his rare find to one of Philip II's official chroniclers, the Cordoban-
born Ambrosio de Morales.[3] He could not have picked a more
appreciative beneficiary. Three short years later the first printed
edition of the Eulogius corpus appeared. As it turned out this timely
publication actually saved Eulogius' literary efforts from oblivion.
By the beginning of the seventeenth century the Oviedo manuscript
had relapsed into obscurity, this time never to be recovered.

At the time that Morales first became aware of the manuscript's
existence he was engaged in the compilation of sources for one of his
pet projects: a comprehensive history of Spain. Eleven years before,
Morales had met some Italian ambassadors in Toledo who were
critical of the Spanish intellectual community for failing to produce
an up-to-date account of Iberian "antiquities and events."[4]
Morales took the criticism to heart and personally resolved to
remedy the cultural defect: "from that point on, I truly prepared
myself for this task, to satisfy this need of my people, and to restore
the honor and authority of our Spain." But, as he soon realized, he
was not alone. A historian named Florian de Ocampo had already
begun a work of similar scope. Yet Ocampo died suddenly in 1563
leaving his magnum opus unfinished and the door open for Morales

to step in. When the Eulogius manuscript found its way into his hands, the task took on an even deeper personal significance. Fifteen years later Morales sent the last volume of his continuation of Ocampo's *Corónica general* to the printers, candidly admitting that no part of the work had given him more pleasure than the chapter devoted to the martyrs. "Because in it I am obliged to write about many holy martyrs through whom the glory of Spain is sovereignly exalted in heaven and on earth, before God and men alike . . . and even more because all of the martyrs were crowned in Córdoba, leaving my homeland illuminated with their worthy triumph."[5]

Morales' pride in his native city as well as in the Spain that had just added a great naval victory at Lepanto to its long list of military achievements against the Muslims on the peninsula, is evident in his manner of presenting the martyrs. His purpose was to bring to the attention of his readers the pathetic heroism of a handful of Cordoban Christians futilely resisting the encroachment of Islam four centuries before the liberation of their Andalusian homeland. Morales made no attempt to recreate the tensions that split the ninth-century community, nor did he dwell on Eulogius' reasons for writing. He simply translated and paraphrased the *passiones* of the martyrs, omitting altogether the lengthy apologies that Eulogius felt obliged to append to them. The seven centuries that separated the two Catholic authors, seven centuries that had witnessed a complete reversal in peninsula hegemony, had removed the need to justify the self-destructive zeal of the martyrs.

Though Morales did not feel compelled, given the sympathies of his audience, to defend martyrdom under non-persecutory circumstances, the awkwardness of the situation was no less apparent to him: "Although the Christians of Córdoba enjoyed the consolation of churches and monasteries, . . . and some liberty to practice their religion, still the greatest and truest consolation, which they had from the hand of our Lord in that time, and the most marked mercy with which he desired to bestow them, was to give them many worthy martyrs."[6] Morales realized that the martyrs of Muslim Spain were not, as their Roman counterparts had been, the product of any obvious form of persecution. But this discrepancy was for him only circumstantial. Divine providence was at work as much in the ninth as in the third century.

Morales' Latin edition of Eulogius' writings and his transcription of the *passiones* in the *Corónica general* assured the martyrs the attention of every subsequent historian of Spain. And every historian who treated the Cordoban executions felt obliged to offer his own opinions as to why, given the lack of persecution, the martyrdoms ever took place.

The most popular means of explaining and justifying the martyrs' actions among Spanish historians, who, like Eulogius and Morales, have traditionally assumed an apologetic stance, has been to question and reinterpret the reputed tolerance of the Muslim authorities. Juan de Mariana, whose *Historia general de España* appeared first in Latin in 1592 and nine years later in Castilian, had to admit on the basis of the surrender terms granted by the Muslim conquerors and Eulogius' references to a thriving Christian church in al-Andalus, that the situation was a "tolerable manner of servitude."[7] But the quality of this servitude was not consistent. Increased taxation under ʿAbd ar-Raḥmān II made life unbearable for the Christians. "From these beginnings, the seeds of ancient animosities began to swell and break open . . . , as the faithful tried to shake off that heavy yoke." At the same time the Christian community of Córdoba became subject to verbal and physical abuse by the Muslim population: "irritated by injuries of this type, the Christians did not hesitate to blaspheme in public the law and customs of the Moors. The kings and governors took this opportunity to persecute the Christian people with the greatest cruelty. . . ."[8]

This reassessment served as the basis of virtually every Spanish treatment for the next 250 years. Enrique Florez, who published his mammoth *España Sagrada*, in 1753, posited the existence of two separate *estados* or "conditions" of Christian life in al-Andalus: one of peace and the other of persecution.[9] The former, as he described it, arose out of a pragmatic realization by the Muslim conquerors that they needed the cooperation of the indigenous people in order to maintain their hold on the peninsula. But just as the references in the writings of Eulogius and Alvarus to a flourishing Andalusian church provided Florez with all the evidence he needed to support the existence of an *estado de paz*, so their reports of taxation and personal abuse suggested a growing *estado de persecución* no less intense than its Roman imperial counterpart.[10]

This emphasis on the persecutory aspects of Christian existence in al-Andalus peaked in the middle of the last century. In a work devoted exclusively to the Andalusian Christians, Francisco Simonet wrote that "Islamization fought with the total weight of its power, with all the rage of its tyranny, and with all the seduction of its sensuality, against the wretched mozarab flock, plotting its imminent and complete destruction."[11] In order to resist this encroachment and maintain the integrity of the Christian community, the leaders had to "apply a moral and superhuman force." They had to defy the persecution and offer themselves to martyrdom.[12] Simonet's definition of persecution, expanded to include not only the "rage" of Islamic tyranny, but the seductiveness of its doctrine and lifestyle, left no room for doubt that the martyrs did exactly what they had to do.

While Spanish historians followed Mariana's lead and portrayed the Muslim treatment of Christians as provocative, a markedly different historiographical tradition developed simultaneously on the other side of the Pyrenees. In 1587, barely a year after Morales released the pertinent volume of his *Corónica general*, a Frenchman from Lyons named Louis Turquet de Mayerne published his own *Histoire générale d'Espagne*. Unlike Morales, Turquet de Mayerne was singularly unimpressed with the zeal that the martyrs demonstrated. His treatment, in contrast to that of his Spanish counterpart, was short and uncomplimentary. "In the end of ʿAbd ar-Raḥmān's reign there was a great persecution against the Christians who dwelt in Muslim territory, the cause of which was their insolence and rebellion." The Frenchman went on to enumerate the various religious liberties that the Christians enjoyed under Muslim rule. Taxes, which the emirs raised from time to time, led to Christian complaint and Muslim irritation. "Some Christians of better judgement exhorted the rest to patience, foreseeing the problem, but it was in vain . . . [as they] were condemned by a council, and are blamed by the authors of histories, who have made no scruple to number as martyrs those rebels who perished in this massacre."[13] For Turquet de Mayerne, the Christians who repudiated the martyrs deserved credit for their admirable restraint and their recognition of the inscrutability of divine providence.

Just as Mariana set the pace for Spanish historians, Turquet de Mayerne's rather deprecatory approach became the norm for scholars who looked at Spain from the outside. The most important of these was the Dutch orientalist Reinhardt Dozy, whose *Histoire des musulmans d'Espagne* first appeared in 1861. Why, Dozy asked, when all the evidence suggested that "the Christians of Córdoba had accommodated themselves quite well to foreign domination," were there "exceptions to the rule?"[14] Dozy offered two explanations. First, priests and monks, who constituted the majority of the malcontents, held extremely biased views of Muḥammad, Islam and the Arab people. They were simply incapable of treating Islam as anything more than a new version of paganism, or of regarding Arab customs as anything less than diabolically inspired profligacy. Secondly, the clerics were sometimes the victims of intolerance at the hands of the Muslim populace, a circumstance which, when combined with such recalcitrant attitudes toward Islam, proved volatile: "Feeling sanctified in their pride, exasperated at the outrages they received, and pushed by a febrile need to act, priests, monks, and a small number of like-minded laymen, would not resign themselves to suffer in silence, to make sterile vows, to be torn with feelings of anger."[15]

The arrests of Perfectus and Joannes were, in Dozy's opinion, the immediate cause of this outburst of "hate and fanaticism."[16] But it was Isaac who provided his coreligionists with a way of demonstrating their discontent in a self-sanctifying way. The subsequent movement not only alarmed the authorities who were, at the time, especially sensitive to any form of dissent, but split the Christian community. Following Turquet de Mayerne, Dozy portrayed Christians like Eulogius' infamous *exceptor reipublicae*, who converted to Islam when faced with the prospect of losing his position, not as bad Christians but as "chrétiens raisonnables" who remained untouched by the fanaticism of the others.[17]

It is not surprising that Dozy's analysis of the situation evoked some harsh criticism from those Spanish historians to whom the martyrs of Córdoba were nothing less than religious heroes and national treasures. Justo Pérez de Urbel, who published a biography of Eulogius in 1927, dismissed Dozy as one "disoriented by his revolutionary and rationalist ideas," and therefore "incapable of comprehending the nobility" of Eulogius' character.[18] On the other hand, Dozy's influence on subsequent historiography is unmistakeable. Modesto Lafuente y Zamalloa, whose *Historia general de España* appeared within six years of Dozy's study of Muslim Spain, admitted that there were fanatics on both sides of the religious division in al-Andalus, and that the hostility that Christians felt toward the Muslims was exacerbated in part "by the sometimes indiscreet and exaggerated religious zeal of some Christians."[19]

But in addition to promoting a greater degree of sympathy for the "chrétiens raisonnables," whom Eulogius had categorically repudiated, Dozy also suggested what turned out to be a very popular way of explaining the harsh reaction that the martyrs evoked from the Muslim authorities. As he saw it, "the Arab government was alarmed with good reason at this new type of rebellion; for among the participants, fanaticism was no more than one aspect of their being; it was mixed with a military ardor and some rather fierce desires for political vengeance."[20] There was, from the perspective of the authorities, little real difference between the spontaneous self-sacrifice of the martyrs and the perennial uprisings by Christian and *muwallad* factions that plagued the outlying parts of the emirate.

Evariste Lévi-Provençal, the great scholarly successor to Dozy, applied this same sort of reasoning in 1932 when he criticized Simonet's religious persecution thesis:

If the reigns of many ʿUmayyad emirs were marked by persecutions of the Christian communities, that of Córdoba in particular, one must realize that these persecutions were dictated less by the fanaticism of the princes than by concerns of a political nature. These communities were in effect the most active focus for movements of nationalism . . . By the force of circumstances, every Christian became suspect; and more times than not this was not without some reason.[21]

The image of the martyrs as early Spanish nationalists proved very popular among Spanish historians of the first half of this century, leading to something of a historiographical *rapprochement* between the two previously antagonistic traditions. Whether or not a state of persecution existed in mid-ninth-century Córdoba was no longer of such pressing concern. The mere existence of a foreign power in Spain was enough to justify the pathetic struggle of the Cordoban patriots.

Pérez de Urbel, who was, as we have seen, less than enchanted with Dozy's attitude toward the martyrs, nevertheless adopted and adapted the Dutch historian's political interpretation for his own biographical purposes. Though no less convinced than his country- men that the martyrs' movement was a reaction against a real persecution, he recognized a nationalistic element, a "tendencia españolista," closely intertwined with the more obvious religious aspect.[22] As Pérez de Urbel saw it, Eulogius "had constituted himself as a leader of a 'national party'" that sought to revive the "old hispano-gothic spirit." "In a time when *españolismo* seemed crushed for good by the violence of the conquering people," Eulogius "rose up bravely with all of the eternal characteristics of his race." As such, Eulogius and ʿUmar ibn Ḥafṣūn, the remark- ably successful *muwallad* rebel of the late ninth and tenth centuries, were two sides of the same coin, both working for the "cause of the Spanish spirit."[23]

This proto-nationalistic interpretation of the martyrs' move- ment achieved its most ebullient expression in the work of Isidro de las Cagigas, whose study of the mozarabs was published in 1947. Expanding Pérez de Urbel's thesis, Cagigas described the Cordo- ban martyrs, ibn Ḥafṣūn, and the rebels of Toledo as three separate manifestations of the same phenomenon: a nationalistic opposition to Muslim rulers on the part of the mozarabs and the *muwallads*, the only truly Spanish inhabitants of al-Andalus. What distinguished the Cordoban situation from the other two was the powerful control exercised there by the emir. The ill-fated revolts of 805 and 818 demonstrated the futility of armed rebellion in the heart of ʿUmayyad Spain. Without recourse to any military option, the Cordoban Christians turned to religion which "opened for them a new road to follow in their protest against the tyrants." In the works of Eulogius, that "revolucionario pacífico," Cagigas found "the first conscious buds of the rebirth of Spanish patriotism."[24]

For all of its attractiveness to a generation of Spanish scholars preoccupied with the roots of their historical identity, the national- istic interpretation has not held up well under the weight of scrutiny. The complete absence of references to any such secular motives in the sources has led J. F. Rivera Recio, Raphael Jiménez Pedrajas, and Emilio Linage Conde to dismiss Cagigas' view altogether in favor of exclusively religious explanations. But what was the precise nature of these religious motives?[25] Over the last thirty years a new generation of historians has directed its attention to this question, from a variety of interesting perspectives.

Franz Richard Franke's "Die freiwilligen Märtyrer von Cordova und das Verhältnis der Mozaraber zum Islam," published in 1953, focuses primarily on the differences between Christian–Muslim polemic in the east and its counterpart in Spain. But in the course of his review of the martyrs' movement, he makes some very astute observations pertaining to the question of motive.

Franke's point of departure is the simple observation that a large percentage of the confessors came from monasteries. Many had, in other words, taken active steps toward detaching themselves from Cordoban society, "to flee from the corruption of the world, a world which bore the stamp of the unbelievers."[26] In addition many of those who had no formal ties to a monastery nevertheless were infused with the same ascetic spirit, and, like Sabigotho and Aurelius, pursued martyrdom out of fear that the usual austerities might not be enough to secure their salvation. In Franke's words, "it must have seemed so much safer to suffer for an instant the surrender to human judgement, to confess Christ publicly and to flee his adversary, and to obtain by means of death the crown of the martyrs, than to run the risk of a lifelong struggle."[27] As we shall see in the final chapter, Franke's emphasis on this link between monastic and martyrial self-denial is the most fruitful approach to the question of motive.

The credit for bringing Eulogius and the martyrs to the attention of American scholars belongs to two historians whose work first appeared in print in the early 1960s. Edward P. Colbert's published dissertation, "The Martyrs of Córdoba (850–859): A Study of the Sources," is precisely what the title states: a review of the Latin documentation surrounding the events.[28] Colbert's specific concerns were, first of all, to search the *corpus muzarabicorum* for evidence as to the state of Christian culture in al-Andalus, and secondly to determine whether or not the victims listed in Eulogius' martyrologies should be considered true martyrs. Despite his expressed intention of avoiding the pitfalls of bias that have trapped previous historians, it is quite clear that Colbert's aim from the outset was to vindicate the martyrs and mozarabic culture as a whole after what he regarded as a century of deprecation beginning with the work of Dozy.[29] The fact that Colbert's treatment offers little in the way of useful interpretive frameworks does not diminish its importance as an exhaustive survey of the primary sources and thus as a catalyst for further research by a broader scholarly community.

If Colbert's treatment can be faulted for its lack of conceptual creativity, Allan Cutler's article, "The Ninth-century Spanish Martyrs' Movement and the Origins of Western Christian Missions to the Muslims," perhaps errs in the other direction.[30] In Cutler's view the martyrs were united in an effort to "create a great rebellion against the Saracen regime in Spain as the necessary prelude to the inauguration of the Messianic Era," by reconverting Christians who had been absorbed either religiously or culturally by Islam. Three characteristics of the situation in Córdoba suggested this hypothesis to Cutler. For one thing, Eulogius' references to Muḥammad as a *praecursor antichristi*, coupled with Alvarus' more elaborate exegetical exercises to the same effect, seemed to indicate a preoccupation, on the part of the martyrs' two main supporters, with the imminent climax of sacred history.[31] Secondly the great anxiety that the movement evoked from the authorities implied that they were extremely apprehensive about the potential for rebellion.[32] Thirdly, the spontaneous confessions of the martyrs resembled the confrontation technique of proselytization that, centuries later, would highlight Franciscan attempts to convert Muslim leaders. "Indeed," writes Cutler, "there is so much similarity between the ninth-century Spanish martyrs' movement and the 'left wing' of the early Franciscan mission to the Muslims that the latter may well have been a revival of the former."[33] We will have more to say about Cutler's thesis later in this study.

As varied as the scholarly treatments of the Cordoban martyrs' movement are, all have two things in common. First of all, in each case the historian has attempted to uncover the single motivating force behind the martyrs' actions, with Muslim persecution, Christian fanaticism, Spanish patriotism and mozarab apocalypticism each enjoying the spotlight at one time or another. Secondly, without exception, they have not hesitated to ascribe the motives of the martyrs to the author of the martyrology. Cutler portrayed Eulogius as one of the orchestrators of an apocalyptic rebellion spearheaded by the martyrs' belligerent proselytization techniques.[34] Pérez de Urbel described him as the "indisputable leader of a heroic event in which two antagonistic peoples clashed."[35] For Raphael Jiménez Pedrajas, Eulogius was the "visible head of the Christian resistance," who sought the same goals as the martyrs: "to provoke in the Cordoban church a healthy reaction, that would free it from the enervating and deadly torpor that was invading it."[36] Neither these historians nor their predecessors seem to have considered the possibility that Eulogius' motives for recording the *passiones* might not be the same as those that led the martyrs to sacrifice their lives. To date only James Waltz and Norman Daniel have recognized the importance of treating Eulogius as a separate entity, apart from the executed Christians whose praise he sang.

Waltz wrote his article in response to Cutler's invitation for "future scholars to dig deeper and come up with better answers."[37] Instead of addressing himself directly to the motives of the victims, Waltz focused on the specific concerns that prompted the literary productivity of Eulogius and Alvarus. Both were, in Waltz's estimation, highly sensitive to the erosion of Latin–Christian culture after almost a century and a half of forced incorporation into an Arab–Islamic world. And both resolved to do something about it. In Waltz's words, ". . . they constructed a positive program designed to uphold the values and demonstrate the superiority of Latin–Christian culture to their fellow Christians."[38] One part of that program involved the revival of Latin scholarship, an end to which Eulogius contributed by securing Latin volumes from the north which had become scarce in the south.[39] Another involved the refutation of heresies, a task which Alvarus assumed with great zeal in his correspondence. Third and finally, both strove for the "intensification of the spiritual quality of Christian life through the maintenance of Spanish Christian practices."[40]

The martyrdoms were not, in Waltz's view, an original part of Eulogius' and Alvarus' program:

Their aims neither required nor anticipated the martyrdoms. Yet it may be argued that they caused the martyrdoms indirectly, because their assertion of Latin–Christian culture in open opposition to Arabic–Islamic culture sharpened the outlines of each culture, made explicit and obvious previously implicit and muted culture conflicts and thereby prepared a confrontation situation in which bearers of each culture maintain the truth of their, and the falsehood of their opponents', faith and culture with all possible reason, authority, and invective.[41]

In other words, the original program of cultural definition and preservation to which Eulogius and Alvarus had dedicated themselves did not include the orchestration of any martyrs' movement. Yet the movement – which may nonetheless have been catalyzed by this program – coincidentally paralleled their program of cultural polarization so that they readily adopted it and incorporated it as a way of "informing, instructing and uniting" Christians against Muslims.[42]

Waltz's contention that Eulogius and Alvarus "had devised and were implementing . . . a careful, comprehensive program calculated to enhance and maintain Latin–Christian culture among Cordoban Christians" places too much emphasis on a single aspect of their literary concerns. By portraying the two as the authors and implementers of a program whose pre-martyrial phase amounted to little more than Eulogius' book collecting and Alvarus' refutation of heresy, Waltz errs in much the same manner as Cutler. Both historians have tried to explain Eulogius' and Alvarus' support for the martyrs in terms of a broad, preconceived campaign, designed to rectify the imbalance between Islam and Christianity. But the evidence required to prove either that they were apocalyptically motivated or that they had worked out a program for the revival of Christian culture is simply not there.

Norman Daniel devoted the second chapter of *The Arabs and Medieval Europe* to the Cordoban martyrs. His decision to ignore previous secondary treatments of the subject freed him from the historiographical labyrinth to make some fresh and useful observations. Most notably he recognized that Eulogius was different from the rest of the martyrs and appreciated the psychological conflicts that surface in his writings. Contrasting Eulogius' enthusiastic support of the martyrs with his personal reluctance to join them, Daniel suggests that Eulogius may have been "just an ambitious cleric who made himself the leader of a party and rose on the bodies of his victims to ecclesiastical preferment."[43] Daniel stops short of subscribing to this hypothesis, taking into account Eulogius' intense personal involvement with some of the confessors. Had he been aware of the difficulties involved in assigning a date to Eulogius' episcopal election – which probably occurred in 852, thus predating the bulk of his literary activity – he would never have suggested it.[44] Nevertheless, as we shall see, Daniel was on the right track. For Eulogius' complex motives do seem to include intense frustration with the local ecclesiastical hierarchy in Córdoba which he perceived to be acting in the interests more of the Muslim government than the Christian community.

The attention of Waltz and Daniel to the mentality of Eulogius and Alvarus, independent of that of the martyrs, constitutes a major breakthrough in approach. Waltz's simple yet crucial observation that the two authors "wrote in response to the martyrdoms," which, as Waltz correctly observed, "is quite different from saying as some do, that they instigated or incited the martyrdoms," underscores an important distinction between the aims of the martyrs and those of the men who chose to bestow sanctifying honors upon them. Because it is, practically speaking, only through the writings of Eulogius that we know anything about the martyrs, it is absolutely essential that we understand the nature of this medium before we attempt to comprehend what drove the Cordoban martyrs to their deaths.

III
Eulogius of Córdoba

4

The life of Eulogius

Of the two men who witnessed and wrote about the martyrdoms, Eulogius is by far the more important source. Though Alvarus' works occupy somewhat more of the *corpus muzarabicorum*, he devoted no more than a single treatise to the martyrs. In sharp contrast, everything that Eulogius wrote dealt directly with some aspect of the martyrdoms.

Eulogius is also the more historically accessible of the two. We have no biography of Alvarus. Aside from the references to his social status and educational achievements to be found in the introductions of letters addressed to him, we are left with nothing more than Alvarus' own writings which reveal little about their author. Alvarus did, on the other hand, have something to say about his childhood friend and lifetime correspondent. His *Vita Eulogii*, together with the bits and pieces of information that we can extract from the works of Eulogius, provide the necessary biographical framework for determining Eulogius' exact role in the events of the 850s.

Still, the information that we have is of rather inconsistent quality. Our knowledge of Eulogius' birth and ancestry is a case in point. According to Alvarus, Eulogius was of aristocratic stock, "born into a line of senators in the noble city of Córdoba."[1] But the biographer noted neither the date of this birth nor the exact significance of "senator" in ninth-century Córdoba. We also know that Eulogius' mother was named Elizabeth and that he had at least five siblings,[2] but there is no mention of his father. On the other hand we know that he had a grandfather named Eulogius who used to cover his ears and murmur a psalm whenever he heard the muezzin's call to prayer.[3] It is possible that Eulogius had some Arab blood in his veins. One of the three confessors to whom Eulogius claimed some sort of family tie was Christophorus, whom Alvarus separately described as *Harabs genere*. But Eulogius admits no mixed blood, nor does Alvarus ever ascribe such an ancestry to him, suggesting that the relative that Eulogius and Christophorus shared was a Latin Christian one.[4]

Eulogius' parents dedicated him to the church of St. Zoylus, where he came under the highly formative influence of Abbot Speraindeo.[5] We know very little about Speraindeo outside of what can be distilled from the praise heaped upon him by his pupils. The only one of his works that has survived in anything but a fragmentary state is a brief response to one of Alvarus' letters describing a local Trinitarian heresy.[6] But all indications point to his example and instruction as seminal in the formation of Eulogius' later attitudes.

Under the tutelage of this man, who was "enriching all of Baetica with the rivers of his wisdom," Eulogius learned the responsibilities of the priesthood and studied the patristic authors available in Córdoba at that time. But Speraindeo's program of instruction also included lessons in the doctrinal differences that separated Christianity from Islam, lessons designed to prepare an Andalusian clergyman for the peculiar demands of a religiously pluralistic environment. By chance a portion of what was probably one of Eulogius' "textbooks" has survived in one of his later polemical assaults on the Islamic conception of the afterlife. Quoting from the sixth chapter of one of Speraindeo's works, Eulogius wrote:

"In the next life," they say, "all the fortunate shall be born into paradise. There God will give us beautiful women, more comely than usual, and ready to serve our pleasure." Response: By no means will they obtain the state of blessedness in paradise if both sexes partake freely in the flow of desire. This is not paradise but a brothel, a most obscene place. The Lord, responding to the Pharisees who had asked whose wife the woman would be upon resurrection who had married seven brothers so that, according to the Mosaic law, she might raise up the seed of the next of kin, said: "You err, not knowing the scripture, nor the power of God. The children of this world marry and are given in marriage. But they who shall be as angels of God in heaven shall neither marry nor be given in marriage upon resurrection."[7]

This excerpt indicates that Speraindeo had composed a lengthy point-by-point rebuttal of Islamic doctrine. As we shall see later,

Eulogius himself frequently resorted to such scripturally-based diatribes against Islam in his attempts to justify the martyrs' actions.

It was in the company of Speraindeo that Eulogius first met Paulus Alvarus, at the time a fellow student. Years later Alvarus would recall his and Eulogius' reckless habit of debating doctrinal issues which they were not yet qualified to discuss, and composing self-congratulatory verse in honor of their naive erudition.[8] As it turned out, neither ever outgrew his love for poetry or his willingness to leave accepted authority behind for the sake of winning an argument.

Although the language of instruction at St. Zoylus' was no doubt Latin, we can be fairly certain that Eulogius could speak some Arabic. Many of the confessors relied upon a speaking knowledge of Arabic to kindle the anger of the magistrates, and it is doubtful that Eulogius was any less exposed to the language than they. At one point the priest even transliterated and translated, for the benefit of his Latin readers, an Arabic prayer used by the Muslims who arrested Perfectus.[9]

When Eulogius achieved *juventus*, he was promoted first to the diaconate, then to the priesthood.[10] Later he became a *magister*, apparently serving in the same capacity as Speraindeo, responsible for the training of young clerics.[11] The only details that we have of this pre-martyrial phase of his priestly life are those relating to two long journeys, neither of which he was able to complete. As Alvarus tells us, Eulogius had always dreamed of making a pilgrimage to Rome, but his responsibilities at home proved far too pressing.[12] He did, however, find time to undertake an expedition north, one which took him to Christian Spain. In a letter of thanks to one of his hosts, Bishop Wiliesindus of Pamplona, Eulogius revealed that his original intention had been to locate two of his brothers who, for some unrecorded reason, had been detained in Bavaria.[13] Upon reaching the Pyrenees, the priest found his route blocked by bandits and the military machinations of one William who, in alliance with ʿAbd ar-Raḥmān II, was fighting Charles the Bald. Carolingian chronicles permit the identification of William as the son of Count Bernard of the Spanish March who had been executed in 844 for supporting Charles' rival Pepin. Following closely in his father's

footsteps, William managed, in 848 or 849, to appropriate Barcelona, which he held until succumbing to forces sympathetic to
Charles early in the year 850.[14]

Hoping to find a safer passage to the west, Eulogius made his way
to Pamplona only to encounter more political instability. This time
it centered around Count Sancius Sancio, whom Eulogius also
described as a rebel against Charles' authority in that region.[15]
Despairing of ever connecting with his brother, Eulogius decided to
make the most of his Navarrese detour by visiting the great
monasteries of the region. He also took the opportunity to collect
some books that were apparently hard to find in Córdoba. Not
surprisingly, given his love of poetry, the titles included many works
by Virgil, Horace, and Juvenal. Far more remarkable a deficiency
of the Cordoban library, however, was that which Eulogius rem-
edied with his acquisition of Augustine's *City of God*. Historians of
Muslim Spain have almost unanimously pointed to the absence of
this patristic standard as symptomatic of the slipping hold that
Andalusian Christians had on Latin Christian culture.

The letter to bishop Wiliesindus, particularly valuable as a
source for students of Spanish monastic history, poses a slight
problem for anyone interested in the precise chronology of
Eulogius' life. Based on the correspondence between the priest's
references to William's civil war and the dated chronicle entries,
Elie Lambert and Léonce Auzias picked 848 and 849 respectively
as the most likely years of Eulogius' expedition.[16] But Colbert has
rightly argued that the year 850, which witnessed the reconquest of
Barcelona by Caroline forces, would fit equally well.[17] It might
even fit better, since the chroniclers both note that William took
Barcelona "through trickery," but lost it in battle, making 850
appear more war torn in the Barcelona area than either of the two
previous years.[18] The determination of the exact year of the journey
is, as Colbert has indicated, important for figuring out where
Eulogius was at the time of the first martyr's death on April 18, 850.
If the priest's problems crossing the Pyrenees were the result of
Charles' efforts to regain control of the Spanish March then
Eulogius was not present when Perfectus was executed.[19]

If Eulogius missed the execution of Perfectus, he seems to have
been back in time to witness Isaac's. He reported to Wiliesindus
that, upon arriving in Córdoba, he "found all things safe and

sound," except that his youngest brother had been removed, for some unknown reason, from the *principatus* by ʿAbd ar-Raḥmān II. But between the time of his return and mid-November 851, when he composed his letter, the situation had changed quite radically:

> We want you, dear father, to be aware of our tribulation, which we suffer these days on account of our sins, so that, defended by the shield of your prayers, we may be led out of this labyrinth of weariness by the unassailable merit of your intercession, which we are confident is worth a great deal in God's estimation. For in the present year, which is 889 *era* [851 C.E.], a fierce, tyrannical madness, rising up against the church of God, has subverted, laid waste and dispersed everything, dragging bishops, priests, abbots, deacons and the entire clergy to prison, consigning them, shackled in iron, to subterranean caves as if they were dead to the world. Among whom I, your beloved sinner, am also confined, suffering all of the horrid squalors of prison like everyone else.[20]

Eulogius transformed his letter of thanks into a prisoner's petition for the type of spiritual aid that the unafflicted monasteries of the north were most capable of supplying.

> This fury . . . has widowed the church of its sacred ministry, deprived it of its oracle, and alienated it from its office, to the point that at this time we have access to no oblation, incense, sacrifice or first fruits through which we might be able to placate our Lord.[21]

Hoping to circumvent this gap in spiritual communication, Eulogius promised Wiliesindus some relics of the Roman martyrs Zoilus and Acisclus to aid in the establishment of a cult in the north that would prove sympathetic to the plight of the Christians in the south.[22]

Eulogius did not explain to the bishop why he and the other equally unfortunate members of the Cordoban clergy had suffered such a sudden turn of fortune. Nor did he mention Bishop Reccafredus, whom Alvarus fingered as the one directly responsible for the arrests. He simply proceeded to describe the heroic efforts of a handful of confessors who, "armed with zeal," had descended into the *forum* to denounce Muḥammad and his followers, without any explicit attempt to connect them to *nostra tribulatio*. Only toward the very end of his letter did he suggest why they had been arrested:

> We believe that we remain bound and shackled for this reason: they think that it was by our instigation, and they ascribe to our instruction, that which these illustrious ones have done as a result of divine inspiration.[23]

This connection between the first wave of martyrdoms and the confinement of the Cordoban clergy provides the only clue as to the date of Eulogius' imprisonment. The radical denunciations that sealed the fates of Isaac and the ten Christians who followed him to their deaths all occurred within the months of June and July 851. There were, according to Eulogius' records, no more executions prior to the very end of his prison term in late November. If the authorities did indeed arrest the clerics because they regarded them as the instigators of the martyrs then we would expect that the roundup of priests began shortly after the two month span of executions, that is, in the late summer or perhaps the early fall of 851.

In his letter to the bishop of Pamplona, Eulogius neither admitted nor denied any personal involvement with the martyrs, but he certainly did not temper his adulation for them. Apparently confident that the new saints could, along with Acisclus and Zoilus, be enlisted to aid the struggling Christian community, he ended his letter with a list of their names and the dates of their deaths, thereby providing the bishop with the minimal biographical information required for the establishment of a new cult.[24]

Eulogius' letter to the bishop of Pamplona was only one of the literary products of his prison months. As Alvarus tells us, the captive priest passed the hours praying, reading, and composing a hortative treatise entitled *Documentum martyriale*.[25] Its purpose was to encourage two fellow prisoners, the condemned virgins Flora and Maria, to maintain their resolve to die for their faith.[26]

Eulogius' prison term also provided him with the forced leisure he needed to complete a project he had begun before his arrest: the *Memoriale sanctorum*. In a cover letter written at some point during his incarceration, Eulogius introduced a copy of this combination apology and martyrology to Alvarus:

> This work was almost finished when an insane decision on the part of the authorities landed me in prison . . . I thought that it would end up dispersed all over the place. But having been preserved at that time by the Lord, now with his help, amidst the anxieties of prison life, it has not only been completed but delivered to you, whom the Lord chose to see it before anyone else.[27]

It seems most likely that Eulogius began writing the *Memoriale sanctorum* either during or very shortly after the first wave of martyrdoms. The fact that he neglected to add any formal closing remarks after the account of Theodemirus' death on July 25 suggests that he was either uncertain at the time whether it would be the last, or that the "insane decision" of Reccafredus preempted its completion. In prison Eulogius met a number of long-time captives who filled him in on the details of Perfectus' passion a year and a half before.[28] He also encountered the merchant Joannes who was still serving his sentence for blasphemy.[29] Thus Eulogius was able to extend his martyrology back in time, providing some precedents for the actions of Isaac and the ten other Christians who died in the early summer of 851. He also seems to have composed at this time the lengthy apologetic preface that would ultimately constitute book one. For when reviewing the types of Christians that had been "sent to heaven by the madness of the gentile mob," he included *virgines* in the company of *presbyteres*, *levitas*, and *confessores*.[30] Since Flora and Maria were the first females among the executed Christians, Eulogius could not have known, prior to their arrest, that they would join the ranks of the other martyrs.

It is difficult to determine precisely when the Muslim authorities first began to single Eulogius out as a dissident supporter of the martyrs. He had been arrested as one of a large body of clerics whom the authorities seem to have regarded more as convenient pressure points for controlling the Christian community as a whole than as actual instigators of the confessors' actions. And he was released on November 29, 851, along with the rest of the detained clerics. As a precautionary measure, the authorities required Eulogius to give sureties that he would remain in Córdoba, but there is no reason to suspect that he was the only one among the prisoners obliged to do so.[31] The "publication" of the *Memoriale sanctorum* after his release was, as far as can be ascertained, his earliest public statement of support for the martyrs. But we have no way of knowing how the work was received by his Christian or Muslim opponents, if indeed anyone other than Alvarus even read it.

Eulogius drew more attention to himself in the months after his release when Reccafredus and the emir began again to apply pressure on the Christian community.[32] Eulogius, "seeing the deceitful strategy of the bishop spreading around him," bemoaned the lack of effective avenues of protest open to him. In an effort to relieve his friend's consternation, Alvarus arranged to have a letter of the fourth-century bishop Epiphanius of Cyprus read in the presence of the Cordoban bishop, Saul. In this letter Epiphanius praised two priests for abstaining in protest from the celebration of the eucharist. Eulogius seized upon the incident as a precedent for suspending himself from performing the sacrament as a means of dramatizing his discontent with the leadership of the Cordoban church. Had the bishop not threatened him with censure, he had, according to Alvarus, every intention of going through with his threat.[33]

No matter how shortlived, Eulogius' refusal to perform the mass was a symbolically pregnant gesture. More than any other ritual, the eucharist symbolized the unity of the Christian community as a whole and the community of clerics in particular. By suspending himself from its performance, Eulogius sought to detach himself from the policies of Reccafredus and those clerics who supported him. Eulogius perhaps expected more support for his action than he actually received. Alvarus was apparently the only one present who could, like Epiphanius, appreciate such a ploy.

This episode was only the first in a series of confrontations between Eulogius and the ecclesiastical hierarchy in the course of the practically martyrless winter and spring of 852.[34] Alvarus recorded that, upon the death of Archbishop Wistremirus of Toledo, the metropolitans and suffragans elected Eulogius to be his successor.[35] But Eulogius never assumed his prestigious new post for "divine providence placed obstacles in his path."[36] Alvarus never let on as to the exact nature of these obstacles. But given Eulogius' outspoken criticism of the ecclesiastical policies of Reccafredus, his apparently open support of the martyrs, and his legal confinement in Córdoba, it is not hard to guess what prevented him from going to Toledo.

The conflict between Eulogius and the authorities erupted once again in the summer of 852. The executions of Aurelius, Sabigotho, Felix, Liliosa, and Georgius on July 27 broke a months-long moratorium on martyrdom and prompted ᶜAbd ar-Raḥmān II to consider a new general incarceration. Eulogius, recounting this episode, wrote:

Learning of this deplorable plan we fled, we departed, we wandered, we hid, and having changed our clothes we made our way in timid flight through the nocturnal silence. We were frightened by falling leaves, we frequently changed our place of residence, we searched for safer places, and we constantly trembled, fearing death by the sword.

This lack of fortitude seems to have bothered Eulogius. But he consoled himself by considering the providential aspects of martyrdom: "perhaps we fled martyrdom not because we feared death, which comes when it will, but because we were unworthy for martyrdom, which is given to some, not to all. Those who have been and are being martyred were predestined from the very beginning."[37]

Though Eulogius was able to ride out this particular storm in hiding, he became a target of reproach during the episcopal council that the emir had convened that summer to consider measures for squelching the new outbreak of martyrdoms.[38] As Eulogius later reported, the *exceptor reipublicae*, who presided over the council, "moved his tongue against me, heaping insults upon me."[39] Recalling the same incident, Alvarus noted more generally that Eulogius was "attacked and irritated by threats" because "he was seen to be the inspirer of martyrdom in those days."[40]

Not long after the council, ʿAbd ar-Raḥmān II suffered a sudden illness which deprived him first of his speech and then, on September 22, of his life. The fact that the attack came when the bodies of Rogelius and Servus Dei were being committed to the flames attested, in Eulogius' opinion, to the "wondrous power of the savior." But his euphoria over what must have seemed to him an all too rare exercise of divine justice was cut short by the accession of the emir's son, who, as we saw in the first chapter, proved to be much more of a *persecutor Christianorum* than his father.

Eulogius regarded the subsequent nine-month hiatus in the martyrdoms as a sign that the new emir's hardline approach had worked. In mid-spring of 853 Eulogius decided to bring the *Memoriale sanctorum* up to date by recording the passions of Aurelius, Sabigotho, and the nine others who had died in the course of the previous summer. He then formally closed the work for the first time with a long invocation to Christ.[41]

Eulogius could not have predicted that within two months he would have five more martyrs to add: Fandila on June 13, Anastasius, Felix, and Digna a day later, and Benildus on the fifteenth. Apologizing to his readers for violating not only the

rhetorical rules against prolixity, but those which frowned on choppy narrative, the priest reopened his hagiographical record.⁴²
There is no way of knowing exactly when Eulogius composed the third book of the *Memoriale sanctorum*. But the lack of any formal ending suggests that this time he decided to leave the register open in the event of more unforeseen executions. Indeed after the five Christians killed in June 853, the martyrdoms did become increasingly sporadic, but Eulogius would never see them subside altogether.

At some point in or after the year 857 the priest composed the *Liber apologeticus martyrum*. Like the *Memoriale sanctorum*, it combined a general defense of the martyrs' claim to sanctity with specific hagiographical narratives, in this case involving the passions of Rudericus and Salomon who died on March 13, 857. In the course of this work Eulogius made passing reference to a new persecution launched by Muḥammad I, made possible by an uncharacteristic lull in the provincial rebellions that plagued the emirate. But the priest did not elaborate.⁴³

We also know from an independent source that in the spring of 858 Eulogius met Usuard and Odilard, two monks from Paris in search of relics. They had come to Spain hoping to secure the remains of St. Vincent, but were disappointed when the Christians of Zaragoza proved reluctant to hand over such a precious spiritual treasure. Hearing reports of an *enormi fidelium interfectione* in process in Córdoba, the two monks decided to make their way south rather than return to France empty-handed. Once in Córdoba, they made contact with Samson, the former translator, who had recently assumed the abbacy of the monastery at Pinna Mellaria. There, as Samson informed them, the bodies of Aurelius and Georgius, as well as the head of Sabigotho, had been deposited almost six years before. The two relic hunters were impressed with what they read in the *passio* and heard from the mouth of Eulogius himself, whose personal knowledge of Aurelius made him an ideal source for additional information about the martyr. Though the monks were very reluctant to part with the relics, Samson and the Cordoban bishop Saul saw to it that the Parisians' detour was not in vain.⁴⁴

As far as we know the *Liber apologeticus martyrum* was the last of Eulogius' literary efforts.⁴⁵ In late winter, 859, the authorities arrested Eulogius for harboring and encouraging the apostasy of the fugitive Leocritia. When questioned as to his motives, Eulogius responded:

The order of preaching is enjoined upon us and it befits our faith that we extend its light to those who seek it from us, that we deny no one who hastens along those paths of life, which are holy. This befits priests, this the true religion demands, this Christ our Lord has taught us: that anyone who is thirsty and wants to drink from the rivers of faith may find a draught double that which he sought. And since this virgin sought from us a rule of the holy faith, it was necessary that we freely give her our attention, that her inclination might be fully ignited. Nor is it right to reject such petitioners, especially for those selected for the service of Christ. Therefore it was fitting that I, inasmuch as I was able, instruct, teach and present the faith of Christ as the way to the celestial kingdom. I would most readily do the same for you if you were inclined to seek the same from me.[46]

The judge reacted to Eulogius' invitation by ordering that he be whipped. But the priest, who had once fled to avoid arrest, was unsatisfied with such a lenient sentence. Now, almost six years later, he told the judge to sharpen his sword and proceeded to point out the errors of Islam. Because Eulogius was such an important member of the Christian community, the judge had him taken to the emir's palace for sentencing by the "royal counselors." There a sympathetic courtier encouraged him to cooperate and avert his own execution:

If stupid and idiotic individuals have been carried away to such lamentable ruin, what is it that compels you, who are outstanding in wisdom and illustrious in manner of life, to commit yourself to this deadly ruin, suppressing the natural love of life? Hear me, I beseech you, I beg you, lest you fall headlong to destruction. Say something in this the hour of your need, so that afterward you may be able to practice your faith. We promise that we will not bother you again anywhere.[47]

But Eulogius chose instead to maintain his course and continued extolling the virtues of Christianity. On March 11, 859, Eulogius was decapitated.

5

Eulogius and the martyrs

What was the nature and extent of Eulogius' involvement with the martyrs of Córdoba? Given the amount of literary attention that he gave to the martyrs, the temptation is strong to assume that his relationship with them was particularly intimate. This, coupled with the fact that both he and his biographer used terms like *incentor* and *instinctus* when referring to his role in the events of 851, have led virtually every historian of Muslim Spain to portray Eulogius as an instigator, whose support and encouragement played a decisive role from the beginning to the end of the martyrs' movement.

But if we look more closely at their use of these terms, we see that they do not bear up all that well under this kind of interpretive weight. Alvarus once wrote that the priest "was seen to be the inspirer of the martyrs in those days,"[1] while Eulogius explained in his letter to Bishop Wiliesindus that he was in prison because "they think that it was by our instigation, and they ascribe to our instruction, that which these illustrious ones have done as a result of divine inspiration."[2] Neither statement sounds much like an admission of guilt. Even on the one occasion when Eulogius actually confessed to having "incited some of them to battle," he immediately confined his use of the verb *incitare* to a rather nebulous "furnishing of arms" for those who, unlike himself, were ready to "fight."[3] The value of such "admissions" for assessing Eulogius' actual relationship with the confessors is questionable. For a proper understanding of Eulogius and the martyrs, we must ignore potentially misleading assumptions about the connections between the two and look at the available evidence more closely.

As we noted in chapter 2, the earliest indication of Eulogius' sympathies for the martyrs are the *passiones* he composed in the late summer of 851, depicting the deaths of Isaac and the seven

Christians who followed in his footsteps. Though it is tempting to date Eulogius' distinctively strong commitment to the martyrs from the moment he began this martyrology, we must realize that such sympathy for Isaac's actions and outrage at his treatment were anything but exceptional during the first few weeks after his death. Eulogius himself wrote that "everyone, cleric and layman alike, greatly angered by the execution, began to extol Isaac's constancy with the greatest respect."[4] When Eulogius began to record the events sympathetically, then, he did so as a self-designated spokesman for these communal sentiments. As a *magister*, and thus one of the leading pedagogical figures of the Christian community, his decision to assume the role of martyrologist would have come as no surprise to his fellow Christians. If we were to use the terminology of the Bollandist Hippolyte Delahaye, we would say that Eulogius simply assumed the traditional role of a *rédacteur*, providing the collective interpretation or *légende* of the events with a standardized literary format.[5]

Nor was this the first time that a Cordoban ecclesiastic had composed a *passio* on behalf of an executed Christian. We know virtually nothing about Joannes and Adulphus, the two Christians put to death in the 820s, except that the man who recorded their deeds, "twinkling like stars in the sky for the benefit of the holy Church and as an example for the weak," was none other than Eulogius' "aged master and illustrious teacher," abbot Speraindeo.[6] The fact that both victims were successfully incorporated into the local liturgical calendar suggests that the abbot composed his account in complete harmony with the prevailing community sentiments.[7] When Eulogius, following in the footsteps of his master, composed the accounts of Isaac and the others, he had no reason to doubt that his work would contribute to the establishment of a similar cult.

But what the priest expected to happen and what actually occurred were two separate things. He did not anticipate the unusually harsh response that the martyrdoms drew from the authorities. Nor did he expect that when ʿAbd ar-Raḥmān II, through Bishop Reccafredus, began to apply pressure on the Christian community as a whole, the unanimity of Christian support for the confessors would dissolve. But in fact many did "change their minds with unheard-of fickleness" and began to condemn the martyrs' actions.[8] Unlike Speraindeo, Eulogius suddenly found his hagiographical efforts undermined, as popular support for the confessors began to disintegrate.

Just as the lack of independent sources makes it difficult to uncover the actual motives of the confessors, so the motives of their detractors can only be surmised from passing references in Eulogius' works. But in the few passages where the priest suggested why the *diffidentes* and *dubitantes* repudiated the confessors, the element he stressed was fear: "everyone was terrified by the anger of the raging tyrant."[9] We have already described the forms that this "iracundia tyranni saevientis" could assume: clerical imprisonment, the expulsion of Christians from public office, and increased taxation. But the real fear was of a more subtle and sweeping nature, a fear which stemmed from the two fundamental facts of Christian existence in al-Andalus: the legal status of the community as a protected but subjected "people of the book," and the socio-economic reality that made inevitable the integration of individual Christians into virtually every corner of Andalusian society. As long as they kept their religious preferences out of the public eye, individuals could, like the merchant Joannes or the *exceptor* Isaac, come to function as highly integrated parts of Andalusian society, perhaps even to the point where certain *dhimma* strictures would be relaxed. Such highly assimilated Christians presumably would not welcome anything that might draw undue attention to their inferior religious status or arouse suspicions about their contribution to Islamic society. The execution of Christians for religious transgressions did not, ipso facto, lead to strained relations between the Muslim authorities and the Christian community as a whole. Joannes and Adulphus apparently died without provoking any official reactions against their community. But the emir interpreted the events of the summer of 851 as a threat that merited sanctions against the Christians as a group. Given the circumstances, any Christian who felt he had too much to lose by being categorically linked to the martyrs had little recourse but to disassociate himself from them by openly criticizing their actions.

The actual size of the Christian contingent that came to reject the martyrs' example is unknown. We would expect to find sympathy for the martyrs in the rural hinterland surrounding the capital, where contact with Muslims was far less a feature of daily life and where the monastic retreats that contributed the bulk of the blasphemers lay. Conversely, the urban Christians who lived and worked in the closest proximity to Muslims, and thereby had the most to gain from cooperation, would be the least likely to applaud the monks' actions once the magnitude of the repercussions became so painfully clear.[10] But the urban–rural division was not hardfast. We know, for instance, that the physical remains of the martyrs were collected by local Christians and deposited in a variety of churches and monasteries in and around Córdoba.[11] But regardless of the relative dimensions of the two groups, the fact that there was community disagreement as to the victims' qualifications bode poorly for their sanctification.

When Lawrence Cunningham recently alluded to a "built-in censorship mechanism" in the canonization process he was referring to the ability of late medieval and modern popes to suppress or promote certain candidates to sainthood.[12] But the same could be said of the *vox populi*, the original, informal "canonization process." Sanctity is a social product, attributed by a community to an individual perceived as having actualized in some particularly meaningful way the values and ideals that inform that community's existence.[13] But if a significant portion of the community fails to appreciate the way in which a candidate embodies those values, any attribution of sanctity will fall on deaf ears. Such appears to have been the case in Córdoba beginning in the summer of 851.

The sudden division of community sentiment left Eulogius in an unwonted position. The hagiographer who had previously served as a mouthpiece for community sentiment now found himself without unanimous support for the praise he had heaped on the victims. Had he confined himself to the strictly representative role ascribed by Delahaye to the typical hagiographer, his composition of the *Memoriale sanctorum* would have ceased the moment public support for Isaac and his followers began to wane. Instead, at what must be seen as the crucial turning point in his life, Eulogius opted to continue on his own, in an attempt to revive and nurture the abortive popular *légende* that lacked the support it needed to survive on its own. The saints' lives that emerged from this single-handed effort had to be more than merely edited versions of collective perceptions. They were, in fact, for lack of a *créateur anonyme*, the creation of Eulogius.

What made this particular Cordoban priest immune to the

reservations of his community? In part the answer is to be found in the intimate nature of Eulogius' relationship with those confessors whom he met prior to their executions.[14] The earliest such encounter took place in a village outside of Córdoba, where the virgin Flora had fled after recuperating from the wounds she had incurred as punishment for her apostasy. Months later, Eulogius would remind her of what for him was the high point of that initial meeting:

I saw the skin of your venerable neck, torn and cut by the lashes of the whip at the time of your persecution; the neck which you deigned to reveal to me . . . And touching it gently with my hand – because I did not think I ought to caress the wound with kisses – I departed from you and for a long time I sighed thinking about it.[15]

This image of a Christian reveling in the presence of a confessor is a familiar one in church history. Imperial Christians frequently lined up at the cells of their condemned coreligionists to solicit personal favors, to alleviate guilt, or simply to bask in the spiritual warmth that they felt emanating from within. To be in the company of such a holy person, or, better yet, to touch the painful "insignia" of his or her office, was tantamout to experiencing firsthand the power of the divine presence. For our purposes, the most significant point about Eulogius' contact with Flora's scar is the timing of the incident, which very likely occurred before Isaac's confession. If, as Eulogius tells us, the memory of his hand touching Flora's scar remained with him a long time afterwards, it may well have served to increase his vulnerability to the power of Isaac's example.

As it happened, this formative encounter with Flora was not Eulogius' last. His subsequent arrest as a cleric and hers as an apostate brought them together once again in prison. This time, however, the spiritual magnetism that attracted Eulogius had been increased not only qualitatively, by the fact that the virgin was even one step closer to achieving her goal, but quantitatively: Maria had joined Flora in her determination to die. Faced with two women on the verge of dying for their faith, he did something that neither Speraindeo nor any of his ecclesiastic forbears for the previous five hundred years had had the opportunity to do: he composed a treatise "in which he tenaciously fortified the virgins for martyrdom and taught them, by means of letters and words, to disdain death."[16]

The *Documentum martyriale* is a textbook example of the hortative treatises encountered in the writings of ancient ecclesiastics who lived during the periods of Roman persecution. As Donald Riddle has observed, the composition of such works on behalf of condemned confessors was one way in which Roman bishops attempted to control the victims' response to imperial pressure, to make certain that they would not vacillate when faced with the ultimate choice of religious compromise or death.[17] The authors relied on a variety of techniques to buttress the confessor's determination to die. The most common was the enumeration of both the rewards that awaited those who endured and the punishments reserved for those who did not. But in addition the confessors were reminded that the whole Christian world was watching and awaiting the outcome of their struggle. This included not only the members of the confessor's community, but also Christ and the other martyrs who resided with him, who had successfully passed the same test and were curious to see if the latest confessors were of the same mettle. The hope was that by recasting the individual struggle of the confessor into a cosmic confrontation between Christianity and its enemies, the stakes would seem much too high for the confessor even to consider relenting to imperial demands.

For the most part, the *Documentum martyriale* followed this pattern without deviation.[18] Eulogius' use of both promises of reward and threats of punishment is indistinguishable from Cyprian's.[19] He also attempted to reduce the chances of a last minute change of heart by putting the virgins' passion in a broader context, specifically by naming the twelve Cordobans who had already met the challenge: "[They] have opened the door to the kingdom for you, preparing a worthy end for your journey, and saying: 'Come, most holy sisters, and enter the chamber of your spouse whom you have pleased thus far in that you fear not to die on his behalf.'"[20]

Eulogius also assured them that their efforts would not go unnoticed among the living. He boasted that, thanks to his literary testimony, "the news of your struggle, passing through nations and peoples, will begin to be known to many."[21] As women they would be providing an especially irresistible example for all Christians, especially those in Córdoba who still hesitated to applaud the martyrs' actions.[22]

Though for the most part faithful to the ancient paradigm,

Eulogius was forced by the peculiarities of the Cordoban situation to adapt or even omit certain time-honored motifs. Cyprian, for instance, could draw the attention of the confessors of third-century Carthage to the tremendous moral support provided by their community as a whole. He could and did make the prospective martyrs feel like local heroes, sacrificing their lives for the sake of their fellow Christians. But Eulogius knew that there was no such universal support for this type of dissent in ninth-century Córdoba Quite the contrary, Eulogius lamented, "[the Cordoban Christians] consider it a delight to be subject to these peoples, and do not resist being led by the yoke of these infidels. They even make use of many of their sacrileges on a day to day basis and seek their company rather than trying to save themselves, like the patriarch Lot, who departed Sodom for the mountains."[23]

Not surprisingly, given the circumstances, Eulogius presented the virgins not as the perfect embodiment of communal sentiments, but as their perfect antithesis. He berated those who would have Flora and Maria "deny and infringe upon their original confession" and impressed upon the two the importance of transcending the general spiritual malaise that had enervated their community.[24]

Eulogius' use of the ancient *exhortatio* genre, then, amounted to more than imitation. Circumstances forced him to adapt the pattern so that it would fit a world in which the confessors lacked unanimous community support. Like the *Memoriale sanctorum*, the *Documentum martyriale* could not simply be an eloquent expression of communal sentiments. It had to supply much of the support structure that was missing in Muslim Córdoba.

Eulogius was by no means unaware of the spiritual benefits he could claim for assisting Flora and Maria in their quests. While the two were still alive he put in his request for the type of aid that only they, as prospective wives of Christ, could provide: "When you approach the chamber of your spouse and obtain in his embraces the fruit of unending union, remember me in your prayers . . . May the succinct mediocrity of this book, which I have written for your consolation, be of some profit to me, a sinner."[25] This is of course a standard motif for this type of composition, making it difficult to assess any special significance it might have held in Eulogius' case. But it should be noted that within a week after their deaths,

Eulogius' fortunes changed so dramatically that he could not resist attributing it to the virgins' successful intercession: "Christ, pleased with their victory and their glorious intervention, removed from us our chains on the sixth day after they were crowned, and released us from prison."[26]

At the same time that Eulogius was composing the *Documentum martyriale* for the benefit of Flora and Maria, he had the opportunity to serve in a similar advisory capacity for another Christian on his way to execution. Aurelius, in the company of his wife Sabigotho, made it a regular part of his self-imposed penitential discipline to visit and console imprisoned Christians. On one such visit, as Eulogius recalled more than a year later, Aurelius "sought my advice about what ought to be done with the property and the children that God had given them; if it was right that the two children be abandoned, whom he was afraid would be given over, after his death, to the profane rite; and if it was right to leave behind such an inordinate amount of riches to be added to the public revenues." Eulogius, faithful to his role as a spiritual advisor to the would-be martyr, "urged him, with regard for the kingdom of heaven and for the sake of eternal retribution, not only to relinquish, but to flee such worldly concerns, and to be mindful of their own souls rather than the welfare of their children." Adopting Christ's admonition, Eulogius bade Aurelius demonstrate the integrity of his desire for spiritual perfection by going and selling all that he had, giving the proceeds to the poor. With regard to the children, Eulogius did his best to console Aurelius by pointing out that their spiritual welfare was out of his hands:

God, who placed them in the womb, is capable of nurturing them from heaven, just as he provides care for all things. Not all little ones are cared for by the industry of parents, nor are they all reared with the labor of a guardian. Man is begotten, and though he may be deprived of the solace of the parent in the cradle, he shall never be deprived of the governance of the Creator, who is the father of orphans and the guardian of widows. O how many children, reared with the delicate care of a parent, come to no good! How many orphans, deprived of any abundance of great assistance, grow up rich in the many things of God, though scarcely able to go on for lack of bread![27]

Small consolation for a bereaved parent, perhaps. But Eulogius' sole concern was to prevent mundane matters from obstructing what he considered to be the holiest of pursuits.

After his release from prison Eulogius met Aurelius again, this time in the company of Alvarus, from whom the prospective martyr had solicited advice of a more general character.[28] Eulogius joined them as they rejoiced over Aurelius' decision to see his quest through to the end. Finally, in late July 852, on the eve of his public confession, Aurelius sought out the priest one last time:

> Before the darkness of the early morning had abated, he visited me again at home to say goodbye, and asked that I pray to the Lord on his behalf, insisting that this act of fraternal charity be made by me, the sponsor of his agony. There, kissing his hands, I obtained his patronage for myself and for the entire Church. After he kissed me in return, we parted in peace.[29]

Within a week Aurelius was dead. Eulogius had once again successfully exercised his hortative function as the *fautor*, or sponsor, of a would-be martyr. But if he was waiting for a sign like the one he received after the execution of Flora and Maria, he must have been disappointed. For shortly after the death of Aurelius, Eulogius suffered, as we have seen, the ignominy of a sharp reproach in the episcopal council.

Eulogius' authorship of the *Documentum martyriale* for the virgins combined with his willingness to advise Aurelius suggests that he was deeply moved by the strength of their resolve to die for their faith. His repeated appeals for saintly intercession imply that he felt a certain security in the power of their martyrial status. If the priest's relationship to all of the martyrs whose passions he recorded had been, as in these cases, one of spiritual advisor, we would need look no further in our search for motives than his initial formative contact with the confessors in prison. But in fact the level of involvement demonstrated in the cases of Flora, Maria, and Aurelius was anything but typical. Of the rest of the martyrs, only Leovigildus, the confessor who accompanied one of Eulogius' martyred relatives, ever asked for and received any encouragement from the priest.[30] Leocritia, whose *passio* Eulogius did not live long enough to write, came to the priest for instruction in the finer points of her new faith, not for advice about martyrdom. In only one other case does Eulogius mention having had any contact with a prospective martyr at all. Georgius, the monk from Palestine who probably met the priest through Aurelius, requested that Eulogius read and forward to his home monastery a brief autobiographical account of his last days.[31]

This paucity of specific references to contact between Eulogius and the confessors does not appear to have been a matter of inconsistency on the part of his records. The pride with which he claimed blood ties to three of the martyrs and a former teacher–student relationship with a fourth strongly suggests that if he had had personal contact with any of the others, he would have been quick to point it out, if for no other reason than to increase the spriritual benefits to which he could lay claim.[32] The fact that he did not suggests that his relationship with Flora, Maria and Aurelius was unique, and that in the great majority of cases the confessors marched to their deaths without the benefit of Eulogius' encouraging words.

Despite the lack of evidence, previous historians have assumed, on the basis of the priest's ties to local monasteries, that Eulogius served in an advisory capacity for many of the confessors. Alvarus did record that his friend "frequently scurried off to the sacred flocks of the monasteries, but lest he be thought to disdain his own office, he always went back to his clerical duties, in which he would persist for some time . . . only to return to the monastery."[33] But even if we could accept this assessment of Eulogius' monastic yearnings as a historical fact, monastic visitation and martyrial instigation are two very separate things. In fact it is difficult, in this instance, to separate the real Eulogius from the Gregorian model of the ideal secular ecclesiastic who, while committed to the *vita activa*, still longs for the purity of the *vita contemplativa*. Like Gregory I, the Eulogius whom Alvarus felt to be worthy of sanctity "would have been involved in both ecclesiastical states if it were possible to do so."[34]

The nature of Eulogius' involvement with the martyrs' movement as a whole is impossible to assess accurately without recognizing how limited his personal contact with the confessors really was. The evidence leaves little room for doubt that in the majority of cases his actual role in the martyrdoms was restricted to supplying the victims with a liturgical afterlife. There is no question that he cheered loudly for the confessors, but, except in a few special cases, he did so from the stands, not from the arena itself.

What, then, prompted Eulogius to defend the martyrs as a group against their Christian detractors? It is important to remember, in this regard, that the clerical arrests served not only to put Eulogius in immediate contact with a very attractive form of religious power, but to taint his opinion of another. For the decision to imprison the clerics was, at least in part, that of Bishop Reccafredus. The irony of a bishop sponsoring the arrest of priests struck a dissonant chord in Eulogius. The letters and treatises he composed in his cell contain cloaked allusions to Reccafredus as the embodiment of a *saevus tyrannicus furor* that was laying waste the church of God, or a negligent shepherd who, far from laying down his own life for the flock, had left it vulnerable to the attack of wolves.[35] Eulogius came to regard the "anguish and imminent dangers" that the "insane decision" of Reccafredus had forced upon him and his fellow clerics, as the marks of an afflicted church in exile. For it was there, in the "innermost recesses of prison," and not in the churches left vacant by the bishop's decree, that the psalms and the "holy murmur of hymns" were to be heard.[36]

We can imagine how his disenchantment with Reccafredus and identification with a captive church could have rendered Eulogius particularly sympathetic to the plight of the three confessors whom he encountered and advised while in prison. The stark contrast between their resolve to die for their faith and the determination of Reccafredus to implement the will of the emir against his own religious community, not only enhanced the priest's distaste for the policies of his superior, but suggested to him a viable medium for expressing his dissatisfaction. By resuming the hagiographical project that his untimely arrest had forced him to abandon, and transforming it into an *apologia*, he could present the confessors as holy antitheses of the destructively conciliatory attitude that characterized the dealings of Reccafredus with the Muslims. Every word of praise written in memory of the victims was a word of opprobrium for the bishop and those who shared his sentiments. Every martyrial image applied to an executed Cordoban carried with it the implicit identification of Reccafredus with the infamous Christians who cooperated with imperial authorities during the Roman persecutions.

The martyrology was not the only medium of protest that Eulogius utilized. As we have seen in the previous chapter, he even considered suspending himself from the priesthood. But, as we have seen, Eulogius was unwilling to alienate the Cordoban bishop. In the end, he would content himself with the literary outlet to which he had already committed himself.

It should be noted that the martyrology provided Eulogius with a relatively safe way of expressing himself. It was unlikely that it would evoke any censure from the authorities. The Muslims apparently did not regard Latin treatises which contained disparaging remarks about Islam or its founder as violations of the proscriptions against blasphemy, because the audience of such works was so restricted. They were written by literate ecclesiastics for literate ecclesiastics. If Eulogius had anything to fear at all it was the reprimand of Christian leaders who did not share his sentiments about the nobility of the martyrs' actions. Eulogius knew this and so dedicated his martyrology to a very specific and sympathetic group: "our holy brothers and sisters in Christ," the inhabitants of the monasteries that had contributed the bulk of the confessors.[37] But others, perhaps, had access to it. It is likely, for instance, that the *exceptor* who upbraided Eulogius in the council of 852 had at least heard about the *Memoriale sanctorum*. But there was little that he could do, for the composition of the martyrology was an accepted, time-honored prerogative of a *magister* of the Christian community of Córdoba. Eulogius made it very clear in his opening remarks in the *Memoriale sanctorum* that he regarded himself as a *praedicator*, a legitimate mouthpiece of Christian truth: "I believe that the same true master who made an irrational animal speak like a man [Balaam's ass], deemed us worthy to employ noble words for the honest instruction of catholics, for the praise of the most worthy saints, and for efficacious attacks on the adversary." Taking it one step further, Eulogius reminded his readers that: "just as it is the duty of those to whom the office of preaching has been given to preach, so it is necessary for you to listen."[38] By introducing the *Memoriale sanctorum* in this manner Eulogius underscored his right to provide laymen with the correct interpretation of the events that had recently divided the community.

If we treat Eulogius' martyrology as a frame for a personal protest against the policies of his ecclesiastical superiors, we can account for many of the discrepancies between the instigator role so often attributed to the priest and those textual references that do not support such an active assessment of his part in the martyrdoms. His limited contact with the confessors makes sense if we avoid the assumption that the author actively encouraged the protagonists of his martyrology. Flora and Maria, two condemned virgins whom Eulogius encountered in prison, were special cases.

Their situation, highly reminiscent of ancient times, evoked from Eulogius an ancient response: the hortative treatise *Documentum martyriale*. In each of the other cases, the advice, instruction, or encouragement that Eulogius gave was in response to a specific request on the part of the prospective martyr. The same can be said for the priest's lack of prescience when it came to predicting new martyrial outbreaks, a curiosity only if one tries to understand his role as more active than it really was. Eulogius simply did not know when to end his martyrology. Twice he had to apologize to his readers for stopping too soon. The only formal conclusion to the work is found at the end not of book three but of book two. Finally this interpretation helps to account for Eulogius' hesitation to join the confessors and seek his own martyrdom. Though he sympathized with the martyrs, he did not see himself as one of them, and openly admitted as much, ascribing his reluctance either to his unworthiness or to the selectivity of the Holy Spirit.

Eulogius was simply not the orchestrator of a "martyrs' movement." For the most part the Christians who sacrificed their lives did so without any of the priest's encouragement. The few with whom he had any meaningful contact, however, made a deep impression upon him, and this, in conjunction with his negative feelings about the leadership of the Cordoban church, accounts for his unflagging literary support of the martyrs as a group long after Christian opinion had turned against them.

IV

The defense of the martyrs

6

Martyrdom without miracles

The manner in which Eulogius defended the martyrs was, of course, largely determined by the specific points of criticism that his opponents raised against them. Those who were unsympathetic were quick to point out that the circumstances surrounding the deaths of Isaac and the rest diverged widely from the pattern set by the ancient martyrdoms. Using the Roman martyrs as a standard allowed the critics to package their criticism of Isaac and the rest in a way that would avert potentially damaging comparisons between their own brand of Christianity and the more "heroic" rendition embodied by the martyrs.

The survival of two passionaries from the tenth century makes it possible to reconstruct the "ideal-type" of the Roman martyr to which the Cordoban martyrs were adversely compared.[1] One *passio* that must have been particularly popular in Eulogius' time was that which commemorated Acisclus and Victoria, who died in Córdoba in the mid-third century.[2] "At that time," the account begins, "the madness of the pagans raged throughout the entire world, so that if one despised the cults of the gods, he would be subject to torments of various kinds." Arrested for claiming that the Roman gods were "nothing but stones, no better than those who worshipped them," Acisclus and Victoria found themselves face-to-face with the prefect Dion, an "iniquitous persecutor of Christians." In an attempt to punish them for their error, Dion ordered Acisclus and Victoria cast into a fiery furnace, only to hear their songs of joy emanating from within. Next he had them bound to stones and cast into the Guadalquivir, only to find them floating on the surface unharmed. Finally he suspended them over a fire, only to have the flames get out of hand and kill hundreds of pagans. Having sufficiently demonstrated both their resolve to remain

Christian and the power that their God wielded, Acisclus and Victoria finally yielded to their would-be executioners and died.

This account of the martyrdom of Acisclus and Victoria is typical of the fifty-two *passiones* contained within the two passionaries.[3] In most cases, the protagonist suffered arrest in the course of an official persecution, repeatedly condemned Roman idolatry, and survived a series of grievous tortures with the aid of divine intervention. Given the fidelity with which each Roman martyr lived up to this stylized pattern and the liturgical regularity with which the Cordoban Christians were exposed to it, the shortcomings of the newest martyrs were all too apparent. Why, if they were legitimate martyrs, were they not subject to any of the insidious tortures that exhausted the imaginations of the magistrates in the passionaries? Where were the astounding miracles that would have protected any true confessors and confounded their enemies? And how could the Muslims be considered analogous to the Romans when, first of all, they were not pagans, and secondly, they never persecuted the Christians?[4]

Eulogius took this challenge seriously and devoted much of the apologetic portions of his work to confronting these specific criticisms. To this end, he had two options. He could question his opponents' interpretation of the events in Córdoba, offering one more faithful to the Roman paradigm. Or he could modify the Roman model itself, by weighing the traditional attributes of martyrial sanctity in a manner more complimentary to Isaac and the rest. In the course of the next three chapters we will see Eulogius moving freely from the one strategy to the other. In the case of the alleged absence of miracles, Eulogius chose a combination of the two.

"If you believe this to be true martyrdom . . . then why are your accomplices neither heralded amidst the terrors of prodigies nor resplendent with signs for the amazement of the crowds?"[5] Eulogius' opponents felt perfectly justified, on the basis of the Roman martyrologies, to expect such signs if the martyrs were, in fact, divinely inspired. For lack of miracles with which to vindicate his martyrs, Eulogius was forced to challenge the assumption that sanctity and miracle working necessarily went hand in hand. Fortunately for Eulogius, he was not the first ecclesiastic to argue this position. Though the circumstances were entirely different,

Gregory I addressed himself to the same issue at the outset of his pontificate 250 years before.

Gregory abandoned the monastic life to become a deacon and ultimately bishop of Rome. Though the papal see was presumably a position that Gregory wanted, it is hard to read his works without sensing a certain defensiveness about having sacrificed the cloister for the world of church politics. In his *Liber regulae pastoralis*,[6] for example, Gregory tempered his praise for monks who placed their own spiritual welfare above service to their fellow Christians: "if they are judged strictly on their conduct, they are certainly guilty in proportion to the public service which they were able to afford."[7] But it was in the *Dialogues*, written three years later, that Gregory expressed at length his opinions about the relative merits of the *vita activa* and the *vita contemplativa*.

Gregory began the *Dialogues* with a rhetorical lament for the peaceful life he had left behind. "At times I find myself reflecting with even greater regret on the life that others lead who have totally abandoned the present world. Seeing the heights these men have reached only makes me realize the lowly state of my own soul."[8] When his literary foil – Peter – asked for examples of such holy men, the pope obliged him with a seemingly endless string of miracle stories. What is interesting about the *Dialogues*, in light of our inquiry, is that Gregory did not really do what Peter asked. He did not restrict his miracle accounts to those involving monks who had "totally abandoned the present world," but included secular ecclesiastics as well. In fact, overall, the miracle-working popes and bishops outnumber the abbots and monks. Gregory's decision to include episcopal miracle workers in a book ostensibly celebrating the *vita contemplativa*, then, apparently reflects a sensitivity to the imbalance between the two ecclesiastical statuses and a desire to correct it.

But this blurring of the distinction between holy bishops and holy monks by indiscriminately ascribing miracles to both was only half of Gregory's strategy to adjust the relative status of regular and secular clerics. For interspersed with the miracle accounts in the *Dialogues* are periodic disclaimers, questioning the need for miracles as indicators of sanctity. At one point, Peter interrupted Gregory's concatenation of tales to ask why such holy men were so rare in their own day. Gregory responded:

I believe there still are many such men in the world, Peter. One cannot conclude that there are no great saints just because no great miracles are worked. The true estimate of life, after all, lies in acts of virtue, not in the display of miracles. There are many, Peter, who without performing miracles, are not at all inferior to those who perform them.[9]

To support his claim, Gregory pointed to the biblical accounts of Peter walking on water and Paul being shipwrecked. "In the very same element, then, where Paul was unable to proceed on board ship, Peter could go on foot. Though these two Apostles did not share equally in the power of performing miracles, it is clear that they have an equal share in the rewards of heaven."[10] In many other places Gregory deliberately directed Peter's attention away from the miracle he had just described to the more praiseworthy humility or patience that characterized the miracle worker.[11]

This depreciation of miracle working may seem, at first glance, out of place in a *libellus miraculorum* like the *Dialogues*. Yet if we recognize that Gregory's intention was to present the episcopacy as an office conducive to sanctity, the paradox dissolves. De-emphasizing miracles served to elevate the traditionally miracle-poor *vita activa* as effectively as any attempt to supply the missing evidence.[12]

Gregory, in other words, had his choice of two paths to follow in his vindication of episcopal holiness. He could either assent to the accepted continuity between holiness and miracle working and proceed to list miracles performed by bishops, or he could reject the one-to-one correspondence between the two and assent to the possibility of sanctity without such signification. The *Dialogues* represent an effort to do both simultaneously. Peter at one point summed up the ambivalent relationship between the two strategies when he said: "I realize now that in these matters one must consider a man's way of life, not his miracles. But since miracles are a testimony to holiness of life, I beg you not to end your narrative. . . ."[13] Gregory did not feel comfortable with any straightforward identification of miracle working with sanctity. To do so would have been to admit to himself that his abandonment of the *vita passiva*, traditionally the more conducive to miracle activity, was a step down. Yet even if every saint did not work miracles, such signs, when present, were still important indicators of holiness, and as such merited record and respect.

When Eulogius' opponents asked him why his martyrs lacked the miracles that would presumably have verified their status, they put him in a position very similar to that of Gregory. He was forced to explain away an apparent lack of miracles without compromising the holiness of his saints. Like the pope, the priest responded by rejecting this one-to-one correspondence. "It ought not to be surprising," Eulogius wrote, "if the martyrs . . . use the power they have received not for their own glory but in the service of their benefactor, if . . . they rejoice, . . . not because they can cast out demons, but because their names are inscribed in heaven." Virtue is what counts. For "both the holy and the reprobate do miracles and prodigies, which confer nothing more than the vain admiration of men. He who thus distinguishes himself may be famous among men, but unless he is righteous he will be condemned to eternal punishment."[14]

Like Gregory, too, Eulogius attempted to correct what he regarded as an imbalance between virtue and power as indicators of sanctity by looking at the martyrs from God's point of view: "He is nothing who is lacking in sincere faith, because God demands nothing else from us than faith." Ultimately, miracles count for very little. "God's witnesses either work miracles or they prepare for death without them. There is no difference. The author of heaven expects only one thing from them: that they consummate their agony bravely to the very end."[15]

Eulogius sounds enough like Gregory to suggest that he may have read the *Dialogues*.[16] If indeed the pope was Eulogius' inspiration, we might have expected Eulogius to follow the pattern of the *Dialogues* even further and argue that in fact the martyrdoms of his day *were* graced with empirical evidence of God's approval. But interestingly enough, he chose not to do that. Instead he accepted his opponents' contention that his martyrs lacked the appropriate signs and proceeded to explain why.

This was not because there was nothing out of the ordinary to report. In the *passiones* Eulogius made mention of a variety of signs that he felt to be indicative of the sanctity of the confessors. The decapitation of Perfectus, which coincided with the festivities marking the end of Ramaḍān, attracted a huge crowd, many of whom took to the river in boats to get a better view. When one of the craft capsized and two men drowned, Eulogius remarked on the speed with which *divina pietas* avenged the death of one of its "soldiers." Eulogius also claimed that in prison Perfectus had prophesied the death of Naṣr, one of ʿAbd ar-Raḥmān II's primary advisors. Within a year of Perfectus' death Naṣr was poisoned. "Thus the Lord, glorifying his soldier with both miracles, strengthened the resolve of the faithful with the solace of great hope, and confounded with a vehement stupor the sacrilegious vanity of the impious."[17]

Eulogius recorded less vengeful signs in connection with some of the other martyrs. On the day of the execution of Emila and Hieremias an unexpected storm darkened the sky, as if to register divine disapproval.[18] Eulogius himself witnessed a heavenly glow emanating from the bodies of Rudericus and Salomon.[19] As we noted above, Eulogius regarded his release from prison as the product of a successful intercession on the part of Flora and Maria.

The remainder of the signs registered in Eulogius' writings could be categorized as portentous or prophetic. Three times Isaac was heard to speak *in utero*, and by age seven, he was experiencing visions that foretold his martyrdom.[20] Sabigotho and Digna also had visions of this kind, and Sisenandus was able to tell his companion in prison the exact moment when the guard was approaching to lead him to his death.[21]

At first it may seem curious that although Eulogius recorded these signs in his *passiones*, he did not refer to them when responding to criticism about the supposed lack of miracles. But there were good reasons for his hesitation. For one thing the signs were very few in number. They were nothing when compared to the endless stream of miracles that filled the pages of the Roman passionaries. Moreover, the miracles that Eulogius reported were not all that unusual. The drownings, the midday storm, and the release from prison were simply not extraordinary enough to forestall more mundane explanations. But perhaps most importantly, none of the miracles that Eulogius mentioned had, like those of Acisclus, ever served to postpone a martyr's fate. They all died with the very first stroke of the sword.

What accounts for the failure of Eulogius' martyrs to provide him with the empirical evidence he needed to make his case? The answer lies in the relationship between the prospective miracle worker and the surrounding religious community. A miracle is an

ambiguous phenomenon, defined not so much by the type or
quality of the event itself as by the interpretation given the event by
its witnesses.[22] The collective mentality of the audience determines
whether or not something miraculous has occurred.[23] If, as was
presumably the case with Acisclus and Victoria, the sympathies of
the local Christians lay with the martyrs, their very expectations
would ensure miracle activity. Over time, as the individuality of the
martyrs became submerged in the ideal of martyrdom, their
miracles would increase in stature and number.[24] The hagiographer, typically composing his text quite some time after the
event, would have no lack of second-hand miracle accounts from
which to draw.

The situation in ninth-century Córdoba differed in two key
respects. First of all, the martyrs died before an audience dominated by assimilated Christians who viewed the confessors' actions
as unworthy of their support, much less that of God.[25] Secondly,
Eulogius often composed his *passiones* within months of the relevant
executions. As a result he could not have profited from any
exaggeration of details even if there had been enough Christians
inclined to nurture the memory of the martyrs.[26]

Eulogius, like Gregory, argued that miracle working was not a
prerequisite of sanctity. But while the author of the *Dialogues* had
been able to say this secure in the knowledge that Italy was
nonetheless full of miracle-working bishops, none of the Cordoban
martyrs had produced a single miracle upon which Eulogius could
make a similar case. The priest, like the pope, knew that in the
absence of such empirical verification there would always be some
room for doubt about the holiness of the martyrs. Always, that is,
unless Eulogius could demonstrate that special circumstances
beyond the martyrs' control precluded the type of miracles with
which, under normal conditions, they would undoubtedly have
been blessed.

Eulogius offered two reasons why the mid-ninth century was not
an auspicious time for such miracles. First he argued that the
church, long since firmly established in the world, no longer needed
the empirical signs that had played such an important role early on.

Truly the Lord performed miracles through his servants at a suitable time
in [the history of] the world since he knew, by means of divine prescience,
that they would have an effect on the people; he knew that those who

worked his miracles would not be acting in vain. And indeed those who had at first rejected the salutary precepts of the sacred law gave way before the wonder of the prodigies. In those times it was suitable for the martyrs of God to shine with signs since they were trying to solidify the original diffusion of Christianity with solid roots in the hearts of the believing people by means of verbal instruction, scriptural exhortation, and the revealing of signs as well as the rewards of passion.[27]

Miracles were a temporary feature of the church, "a tool of iron by which ornaments of gold and silver were formed, joined, fitted and fashioned into necklaces, collars, and diadems for kings."[28] In and of themselves they were worthless and disposable the moment they had served their purpose.

This was by no means a new argument. The early Christian apologists, in their efforts to defend Jesus against accusations of sorcery, had to downplay his miracles. Origen was one of the first to suggest that these displays of supernatural power had never been intended to serve any broader function than that of leading the first generation to the "wonderful teachings of the gospel," which alone could effect the truly noteworthy miracles of making spiritually blind men see and spiritually lame men walk.[29] Later Augustine took the same position in order to allay the fears of his congregation that Christ, whose miracle activity was limited to the earliest years of the Church, held the Christians of later ages in less regard. But Augustine could claim that miracles were not necessary while secure in the knowledge that they were, in fact, occurring daily at the shrines of St. Stephen.[30] Again, Eulogius had no comparable signs to fall back on. All he could do was to build as strong a case as possible for the general absence of miracles in his own day.

Eulogius supplemented his argument that miracles properly belonged only to the *primordium* of church history, with a variation on the same theme borrowed from Gregory's commentary on Job. "Prior to the appearance of the Leviathan . . . miracles will be removed from the holy Church . . ." No longer will the "divine dispensation . . . make itself known openly and repeatedly." The purpose, according to Gregory and Eulogius, was simply to separate the sheep from the goats: "the reward of the good who venerate the Church because of their faith in heavenly things and not because of present signs shall increase," while those who demand miracles will expose the superficial quality of their faith.[31] This apocalyptic approach served Eulogius' purposes rather nicely, for it was precisely this "faith in heavenly things" without signs that the priest was trying to engender for the sake of the martyrs.

If such temporal restrictions were not enough, Eulogius relied on his own exegesis to provide a fascinating geographical one, which specifically precluded the possibililty of such signs occurring in Muslim Spain:

> Not everyone is worthy of contemplating heavenly powers, as can be easily shown by looking at the apostolic miracles. When the apostles wanted to preach the gospel to the Asians, they were prevented by the Holy Spirit, which, when long ago it began to spread the gospel, knew that no one worthy of receiving the evangelical truth existed in Asia, and rightly prevented the disciples by the prophetic authority of divinity.[32]

Only peoples originally designated "convertible" by the Holy Spirit could expect divine signs to testify to the truth of the Christian message. Eulogius considered groups like the Asians, and by extension the Andalusian Muslims, to be hopeless cases on which God would not waste his precious signs.

By precluding the possibility of miracle activity in ninth-century Córdoba, Eulogius defused his opponents' contention that a lack of signs was a reflection of the martyrs' status in God's eyes. What his opponents had used as evidence for repudiating the martyrs, Eulogius transformed into nothing more than a sign of the times and a reflection of geographic circumstances that had no bearing whatsoever on the status of the martyrs.

Had Eulogius fully worked out the implications of what he was saying, he might have realized that he had strained at a gnat only to swallow a camel. His argument, elevating the problem of miracles from his martyrs to the Andalusian church as a whole, succeeded in its designated purpose: it prevented the lack of miracles from being used against his martyrs. But Eulogius was prepared neither to follow up his apocalyptic explanation with prophecies of an imminent historical climax, nor to square the proscription against preaching the gospel in "Asia" with the continued existence of a Christian community in al-Andalus. We will never know if these problems bothered Eulogius. But the absence of any trace of uneasiness suggests that his efforts to vindicate the Cordoban martyrs engaged him so completely that any dubious implications of an otherwise useful argument could be brushed aside in the interests of the more pressing matter at hand.

7

Martyrdom without pagans

That the types of miracles that would have vindicated the martyrs did not occur is symptomatic of the mixed sentiments of the Cordoban Christian community. Direct pressure from the Muslim authorities no doubt contributed to the antipathy toward the martyrs. But again the fear of repercussions was neither the only nor even the most significant deterrent to local sympathy for the martyrs. As we suggested above, the religiously pluralistic environment of al-Andalus and the political domination of Muslims had, over time, a definite impact on the attitudes of the more assimilated Christians in the city. Consciously and unconsciously individual Christians learned how to balance the cooperative attitudes that would facilitate their incorporation into Andalusian society with their ongoing need to preserve their religious identity.

The repercussions of this process are perhaps nowhere more apparent than in the second of the objections raised against the martyrs. For in addition to the lack of miracles, Eulogius' opponents objected that his martyrs "suffered at the hands of men who venerated both God and a law and were not killed as ones summoned to sacrifice to the idols . . ."[1] Again the point was to discredit Isaac and the rest by contrasting the circumstances of their deaths with those of their ancient counterparts. But this time the issue was the character of the persecutors, not the victims. The Roman prefects were pagans who implemented sacrificial tests of imperial loyalty, leaving the ancient Christians no choice but to resist and denounce the Roman gods. On the other hand the Muslims, as Eulogius' opponents correctly observed, were monotheists who worshipped the same God as they, though living according to their own revealed law. This was, for the assimilated Christians, a very important difference. As far as they were concerned the fact that Islam was not a pagan religion served both to legitimate their cooperative attitudes toward the Muslims and to render inappropriate the radical attitudes of the confessors.[2]

This emphasis on the common ground shared by Islam and Christianity as a basis for coexistence was no doubt inspired by traditional Islamic attitudes toward Christianity and Judaism. Because the Muslims considered Muḥammad the last recipient of a long series of revelations beginning with those experienced by Abraham, they tended to stress the continuity of revealed truth and the consistent quality of its spokesmen. Perfectly cognizant of the unity of God, Moses and Jesus were as "muslim" (literally, "one who submits" to Allah) as Muḥammad ever was. This respect for the pre-Muhammadan prophets manifested itself in the special treatment accorded to "peoples of the book" who, though suffering from the effects of corrupted texts, were nevertheless united in their recognition of the one God. The same perspective that governed Muslim relations with *dhimmī* populations provided subject Christians with a natural, pre-packaged way of justifying Christian interaction with, and assimilation into, the Islamic society of ninth-century Córdoba. It was the common religious denominator that mattered. The significance of the countless differences in belief and ritual that separated the two religions paled by comparison.

But if this perspective helped alleviate anxiety among the Andalusian Christians who worked and lived in close proximity to Muslims, it did so only at the cost of suggesting that, among other things, the Christological differences that separated Christianity and Islam were relatively insignificant. To argue against the sanctification of the martyrs on the basis of their religious kinship to their executioners, was to imply that the confessors, by merely testifying to the divinity of Christ, had not picked a sufficiently important point of doctrine to merit their self-sacrifice.

Not surprisingly, given his *raison d'écrire*, this type of "ecumenical" attitude toward Islam was entirely unacceptable to Eulogius:

Those who assert that these soldiers [martyrs] of our own times were killed by men who worship God and have a law, are distinguished by no prudence with which they might at least give heed to cautious reflection, because if such a cult or law is said to be valid, indeed the strength of the Christian religion must necessarily be impaired.[3]

Quoting from Paul's letter to the Galatians – "If anyone preach to you a gospel besides that which you have received, let him be anathema" – Eulogius underscored the exclusivity of Christianity, which, as he saw it, had "penetrated every corner of the world and traversed every nation on earth."[4] This left no room, according to Eulogius and Paul, for any new law modifying the one brought by Christ. For a Christian to claim that a more recent revelation had any validity at all was to fail to appreciate the universality of the gospel. Besides, Eulogius asked,

What is the purpose of believing that a demoniac full of lies could speak the truth? that one enveloped in fallacies could provide a law? that a perverse grove could produce good fruit? In the meantime, that abominable one brings evil from the terrible treasure of his heart, and offers a wealth of impiety to the foolish crowd, so that both he and they are cast down into the eternal void.[5]

In reaction to what he saw as a dangerous tendency to downplay the differences between the two religions, Eulogius offered his own interpretation of Islam, one that he felt would justify the martyrs' actions. To begin with, Eulogius had to make it very clear that the differences between Islam and Christianity were not as minor as many of his fellow Christians pretended. Muḥammad, he wrote, "teaches with his blasphemous mouth that Christ is the Word of God, and his Spirit, and indeed a great prophet, but with none of the power of God, like Adam, not equal to God the Father."[6] By focusing his readers' attention on the central difference between the two religions, Eulogius not only underscored the carelessness of his opponents, but, more specifically, reminded them of the Christological parallels between Islam and Arianism. This in turn opened the door to an ancient stockpile of readily adaptable polemical ammunition to use against Islam.[7]

Just as Hilary of Poitiers, the principal Latin polemicist in the struggle against Arianism, hyperbolized the doctrinal deviance of Arius, transforming him into the most infamous of heresiarchs, so Eulogius placed Muḥammad at the apex of error:[8]

Of all the authors of heresy since the Ascension, this unfortunate one, forming a sect of novel superstition at the instigation of the devil, diverged most widely from the assembly of the holy church, defaming the ancient authority of the law, rejecting the visions of the prophets, trampling the truth of the holy gospel, and detesting the doctrine of the apostles.[9]

Like Hilary, Eulogius also made good use of the image of the false prophet, the coming of which Christ had foretold to the apostles.[10]

Three characteristics of the false prophet, as depicted in the gospels and the epistles, seemed, in Eulogius' opinion, to fit Islam's prophet like a glove. First of all, it made sense chronologically because Muḥammad had experienced his visions some 600 years after Christ had closed the door behind him to any modification of his message. Secondly, it fit in terms of the sheer numbers of Muslims that had occupied the eastern, western, and southern shores of the Mediterranean, for Christ had specifically warned his followers that *many* would be led astray by such "ravenous wolves in sheep's clothing."[11] Finally, the "false prophethood" of Muḥammad provided an explanation for both the existence of recognizably Christian themes within his doctrinal scheme, and their modification at his hands. It made sense that a false prophet, surfacing in the wake of Christian missionary success, would incorporate twisted versions of the more salient aspects of Christianity to "season his error," making it more attractive to prospective converts. This allowed Eulogius to account for, among other things, the Qur'anic afterlife: Muḥammad had adopted it from Christianity, but had adapted it to meet his own lusty needs until it resembled a brothel.[12]

In terms, then, of the chronology of the two religions, the great number of Muslims, and the Christian doctrinal resonances within Islam, the New Testament image of the false prophet suited Islam. It thus provided Eulogius with the perfect way of sidestepping the criticism that Islam, as a religion that recognized the Christian God, did not merit the radical denunciations pronounced by the martyrs. Though admitting that Muslims were not pagans, the priest could nevertheless chastise his fellow Christians for allowing themselves to be led astray by one of the false prophets that Christ had predicted would emerge in his absence.

But if Eulogius selected this model because it made sense out of the readily observable characteristics of Islam in the ninth century, he also realized that it would provide him with a polemically useful way of assessing the character and motives of the movement's founder. For it made sense to him to describe the false prophet, defined as the perfect antithesis of the true prophet, as a parody of his holy counterpart. Inasmuch as John the Baptist, in the well-worn pattern of the Old Testament prophets, rejected all material things, living on locusts and honey in the wilderness, his antithesis would be expected to embrace every polluting aspect of the world.

Similarly, if the source of John's inspiration and the force that moved his lips was God, the devil had to be the one behind Muḥammad's fabrication of revelation. If, in short, it made sense to see Islam as a false prophecy, then it made sense to see its founder as a diabolically inspired profligate.

The words that Eulogius put into the mouth of the priest Perfectus illustrate how he made polemical use of the contrast between the probity of the true prophet and the supposed degeneracy of Muḥammad:

In what manner can he be considered one of the prophets, how can he avoid being punished by a curse from heaven, who, blinded by the beauty of Zainab, the wife of Zaid, one of his countrymen, and taking her on the basis of some barbaric law, as if an irrational horse or mule, joined himself to her in adultery, and claimed to have done it at the command of an angel?[13]

Moreover, Eulogius never stopped reminding his readers of the evil source of Muḥammad's inspiration:

O head empty of brains and heart occupied with the privilege of Satan! O corrupt vessel and abode of unclean spirits! O tongue worthy of being cut in two by a sword! O instrument of the demons and symphony of the devil! What madness and insanity compel you to be polluted with such blasphemies? What, O sewer of filth, snare of perdition, abyss of iniquity and cesspool of all vice, has deprived you of your human senses?[14]

Eulogius' task in transforming Muḥammad into a false prophet was simplified by the discovery, during his sojourn in northern Spain, of a short account of the prophet's life buried away in the monastic library of Leyre near Pamplona.[15] The anonymous author described Muḥammad as an "avaricious usurer" working for "a certain widow" whom he later married "by some barbaric law." During his business trips, he began to attend Christian church services and memorize the sermons he heard, thus becoming "the wisest of all among the irrational Arabs." Subsequently he experienced diabolic visions of a golden-mouthed vulture – an apparent parody of the dove that traditionally represents the Holy Spirit – claiming to be Gabriel. The vulture commanded Muḥammad to pass himself off as a prophet, which proved an easy thing to do given the lack of sophistication of his pagan audience. And "he made headway as [the Arabs] began to retreat from the cult of the idols and adore the incorporeal God in heaven." He then commanded them to fight on his behalf and they succeeded in defeating the Byzantine forces and establishing Damascus as their capital. Acting as a prophet, Muḥammad fabricated "psalms" – the ṣūras of the Qur'ān – about various biblical figures as well as animals, birds, and insects. He also instituted a law that allowed him to exercise his lust on Zainab, the repudiated wife of Zaid. He prophesied that after his death he would rise after three days, but when the time came, he instead lay rotting until his stench attracted a pack of dogs. His followers buried what remained of his body and conspired to conceal the truth concerning his demise. "It was right that a prophet of this kind fill the stomachs of dogs, a prophet who committed not only his own soul, but those of many, to hell."

It is not difficult to understand why Eulogius incorporated this text into his argument. For while it clearly stated that Muḥammad "made headway" in directing the Arab idolators toward God thereby conceding the monotheistic common ground of Christianity and Islam, it nevertheless left no doubt that the latter was a diabolically inspired product of a moral reprobate that merited the strongest repudiation.

Aside from "heresiarch" and "false prophet," Eulogius also applied the label "antichrist" to Muḥammad, who, like Arius, earned the ignominious title by refusing to accept the divinity of Christ. Yet while Eulogius used the term *praecursor antichristi* interchangeably with *pseudopropheta* in reference to Muḥammad, he passed up the opportunity to elaborate. Why? Because Alvarus was already working on just such an interpretation. The entire second half of the *Indiculus luminosus*, Alvarus' sole contribution to the defense of the martyrs, was dedicated to a line-by-line commentary on the passages in Daniel and Job that had traditionally been regarded as references to antichrist.

Alvarus began with the description of the fourth beast found in Daniel:

The fourth beast shall be the fourth kingdom upon earth, which shall be greater than all the kingdoms, and shall devour the whole earth, and shall tread it down, and break it into pieces. And the ten horns of the same kingdom shall be ten kings: and another shall rise up after them, and he shall be mightier than the former, and he shall bring down three kings. And he shall speak words against the High One and shall crush the saints of the most High: and he shall think himself able to change times and laws, and they shall be delivered into his hand until a time, and times, and half a time.[16]

Alvarus' interpretation of this passage followed the official patristic version only insofar as it identified the fourth beast as Rome. Thereafter creative substitution was the rule. The eleventh horn, "which everyone throughout history has identified . . . as Antiochus," the most likely candidate given the time in which the book of Daniel was composed, became a symbol for Muḥammad.[17] Accordingly, Alvarus identified the three displaced kings as the rulers of the Greeks, the Visigoths, and, for less historical reasons, the Franks. The words spoken against God, the crushing of the saints, and the fabrication of law required no great feats of exegetical dexterity to make them fit the *vates nefandissimus* of Islam. Alvarus even offered his own guess as to when Islam's time would run out. Making use of the reference in Psalm 89, he algebraically substituted seventy years for each of the three and one half "times" and calculated that the end would come after 245 years of Islamic rule, that is, as he figured it, in the year 870.[18]

Alvarus then moved on to Daniel 11. He quickly demonstrated how Muḥammad had spoken "great things against the God of gods," and identified the god Maozim of the prophecy with the deity whom the Muslim muezzins venerated from the "fuming towers" of the mosques.[19] Coming to the passage, "and he shall follow the lust of women," Alvarus launched into a tirade against Muḥammad's sexuality, transforming him into a libertine worshipped by adulterous Arabs for his unmatched sexual prowess.[20] Moreover, he ridiculed the paradise of the Qur'ān, depicting it as a supernatural brothel.[21]

Alvarus ended his treatise with another commentary, this time on Job 40 and 41. Gregory's classic interpretation of the behemoth and the leviathan as prefigurations of antichrist suggested to Alvarus the connections between the beasts and Muḥammad. He found passages which seemed appropriate expressions of the shallowness of Islamic culture, the demonic source of Muḥammad's inspiration, and the relentless ruin of ignorant Arab souls. He also found verses which put the problems of mid-ninth-century Córdoba in biblical perspective. The leviathan, breathing fire and belching smoke, and the behemoth, "wielding his tail like a cedar," embodied the persecuting force which Christians, like the confessors, did well to combat.[22]

There is every reason to believe that Eulogius not only knew of, but applauded, the work of his friend. He may even have commissioned it, for both the initial apologetic portions of Eulogius' martyrologies and the first half of Alvarus' work decry the same lack of community support for the martyrs, inveigh against the same types of oppression, and laud the same zeal of the confessors. Alvarus' purpose was much the same as that of Eulogius: to present Muḥammad and Islam in such a way as to justify the martyrs' suicidal behavior.

To date, the scholars that have given their attention to these specific characterizations of Islam and its prophet have had difficulty keeping this apologetic context in mind. This has led to some potential misconceptions about, for one thing, the supposed apocalypticism of Eulogius and Alvarus. R. W. Southern, for instance, described the two as "inspired by the idea that the rule of Islam was a preparation for the final appearance of Antichrist."[23] And Allan Cutler, as we have seen, went so far as to explain the actions of the confessors and the writings of Eulogius and Alvarus in terms of their supposed messianic expectations.

The fact that Eulogius used the term *praecursor antichristi* without even alluding to its apocalyptic implications is difficult to explain if he really was convinced that the martyrs were engaged in some sort of cosmic millenarian conflict. Even Alvarus, who spilled a great deal of ink substituting Muḥammad for Antiochus, the behemoth, and the leviathan, carefully avoided extending the analogy to any speculation about the nature of the new age or the events that would usher it in. It is true that he offered his own estimate of the amount of time that Islam, as a political power, had left. But having arrived at a date, he immediately shifted his attention to a lengthy apology for undertaking a scriptural interpretation that contradicted Jerome. By so doing, he cut off his treatment of Daniel 7 after verse 25, leaving the succeeding passages, which pertained to the rendering of judgement after the fall of the eleventh horn, untouched. It would seem that Alvarus regarded the numerical calculation, like the identifications of the three displaced kings, as just one more means of identifying Muḥammad with the Danielan antagonist, so that he could take advantage of the passages that seemed particularly appropriate for riddling Muḥammad's character.

Alvarus' choice of apocalyptic texts is also indicative of his restricted intentions. Job 40 and 41 contain nothing but detailed descriptions of the physical and behavioral characteristics of the two monsters, and as such, served perfectly the needs of an exegete looking for a biblical portrait of Muḥammad but unconcerned with the details of the conflagration. Revelation was the obvious choice of texts for anyone trying to relate biblical eschatology to contemporary events, and Alvarus, aside from a short reference to Christians who bore the "mark of antichrist" by fraternizing with Muslims and becoming absorbed in Arabic culture, completely ignored it.

The strongest evidence against the attribution of any special apocalyptic sentiment to Alvarus, however, is the manner in which he vindicated his exegetical novelty in light of existing patristic interpretations: "I believe Antiochus, Nero, and all the others whom the blessed doctors reveal, to be confirmed precursors of antichrist. They would also consider Muḥammad to be an instrument of antichrist if they could be here in our own times." Continuing in the same vein: "Jerome said that there were many antichrists, and we have seen what the apostle John preached. Whosoever, then, denies Christ as proclaimed by the apostles is an antichrist."[24] These passages suggest that Alvarus' decision to describe Muḥammad as a *praecursor antichristi* did not necessarily mean that he anticipated the end of the world. There had already been many such figures, and Alvarus, by imputing such characteristics to Muḥammad, was simply adding one more to the list.[25]

Just as the point of Alvarus' exegesis was not to equate Muḥammad's efforts with those of the ultimate antichrist of Revelation but, more generally, to portray him and his religious legacy as anti-Christian, so Eulogius' use of the Leyre biography is not necessarily indicative, as historians have claimed, of the extent of his knowledge of Islam. Dozy, in reference to the Cordoban clergy as a whole, wrote:

Living in the midst of the Arabs, nothing would have been easier than to instruct themselves [about Muḥammad and his teachings]; but, obstinately refusing to partake of the resources that were to be found at their very doorsteps, they preferred to believe and repeat all the absurd fables that were reported elsewhere about the Prophet of Mecca.[26]

Building on the same observation, Southern regarded the priest's preference "to know about Muhamet from the meager Latin source which Eulogius found in Navarre, rather than from the fountain-head of the Koran . . ." as symptomatic of a xenophobic ignorance, which characterized early Spanish views of Islam in general.[27] Finally, in the course of his recent study of cultural interaction in medieval Spain, Thomas Glick treated Eulogius' reliance on a "debased, distorted Latin version" of Muḥammad's life found in Navarre as an "apt example of the cultural isolation of the Latin mozarab writers."[28]

It is possible that Eulogius did subscribe completely to the Leyre account of the life of Muḥammad. The fact that he, like his Christian opponents, knew enough about Islam to distinguish it from paganism would not necessarily preclude ignorance about the details of the prophet's life. But given the fact that Eulogius had polemical reasons for using a biography that not only filled out his identification of Muḥammad and the *pseudopropheta*, but added the weight of authority to his interpretation, we cannot simply assume that he considered this account accurate. We have already seen, in the previous chapter, that Eulogius' determination to defend the martyrs led him to offer a variety of explanations for the lack of miracles without fully considering the implications of his arguments. The same determination may account for his decision to use the Leyre account, not because it most accurately reflected his own understanding of the origins of Islam, but because it most effectively served his apologetic purposes.

8

Martyrdom without persecution

The fact that the Muslims worshipped one God was not the only thing that distinguished them, in the eyes of Eulogius' opponents, from the ancient authorities. The manner in which they treated the Christians also differed. For one thing, as the detractors observed, the Romans "harassed the Christian soldiers who resisted and fought them with insults, afflictions, lashes, gibbets, flames, beasts, drownings, and various other kinds of torments, hoping, by means of punishment, to recall their souls from the practice of their religion . . ." In contrast these "soldiers and confessors of our day, receiving a speedy death at the edge of a sword, have not had to perspire under protracted torments or to endure any of the bitterness of fierce torture."[1]

There was no denying that the Cordoban martyrs were spared the elaborate tortures that filled the pages of the Roman passionaries. Examples of mistreatment by the Muslims were in fact rare enough for Eulogius to register his surprise when they occurred. As the priest reported in the *passio* of Isaac, Muslim officials restrained and chastised the *qāḍī* who struck the blasphemous monk. For, Eulogius observed, "according to their law, he who, as a result of his crimes, merits death, ought not to be subject to any physical abuse."[2]

If Eulogius had to admit that the martyrs suffered little prior to their executions, he could and did question the importance of torture in the long run. "What does it matter if one perishes after extended torture or with a sudden stroke, when the same zeal for God and the same love of the eternal kingdom crowns both?" Moreover, his opponents were forgetting how awful a thing death in itself really was. "What among all the punishments," asked Eulogius, "is more cruel than death? What is more terrible than to see in plain view the quivering sword ready to fall on the neck of the confessor?" The only meaningful criterion for evaluating a given death was the end for which it was endured, not the means by which it was accomplished. "Death may come quickly or slowly; what matters is whether they suffered their passions for the sake of the faith, whether they strove to lose their lives on behalf of Christ, the one who crowns martyrs, so that they might be saved."[3] As Eulogius saw it, there was no glory inherent in mutilation. The quality of one's intention was all that really mattered. Like the thief on the cross, the martyrs could expect to be judged not in terms of the circumstances that led to their deaths, but in terms of the degree of their commitment to Christ.

More problematic for Eulogius than the lack of torture was the absence of a general persecution that would have helped justify the actions of the martyrs. The vast majority of the ancient martyrs whose deaths were celebrated liturgically in ninth-century Córdoba died during designated periods of persecution, particularly under Decius in the mid-third century and Diocletian in the early fourth. Typically, as in the case of Acisclus and Victoria, the local magistrates sought out and arrested recalcitrant Christians, ordered them to venerate the imperial deities, and punished their refusal with torture and execution. In marked contrast, Isaac and most of the others who followed came forward, unsummoned and without any pressure to forsake their religion, to denounce Islam in deliberate violation of the laws against blasphemy. Paraphrasing the sentiments of his opponents, Eulogius wrote: "No violence compelled them to deny their faith or forced them away from the practice of the holy and pious religion; but giving themselves over to destruction of their own free will and on account of their pride – which is the beginning of all sin – they killed themselves and brought about the parricide of their own souls."[4] By so doing they had proved themselves unworthy of the ranks of the Roman martyrs.

The points at issue were actually two: the excessive volition that characterized the confessors' pursuit of martyrdom and the lack of provocation on the part of the authorities. In both cases Eulogius chose to deny his opponents' observations, claiming on the one hand that the zeal of the martyrs was no more excessive than that of some of the Roman confessors, and on the other that a state of persecution did indeed exist in Córdoba in their own time.

The precise boundaries of acceptable volition on the part of a Christian facing execution had never really been established during the martyrial phase of church history. No one doubted that will was a necessary component of proper martyrdom. The victims of the Roman persecutions were glorified by the surviving Christians precisely because, when faced with a choice between life and death, they chose their own destruction. The question was not, therefore, whether individual will played a part in martyrdom, but rather how much will a prospective martyr ought to exercise in securing his goal.

Two of the earliest recorded martyrdoms illustrate the wide latitude of opinion on the matter. In the early second century Ignatius of Antioch presented himself as a Christian to Trajan, knowing full well that his admission would lead to the amphitheatre. Writing to dissuade the senate from remitting his sentence, he pleaded lest any "unseasonable show of good will" on their part prevent him from being "ground by the teeth of the wild beasts" and thus being transformed into the "pure bread of Christ."[5]

The intensity of Ignatius' desire to undergo any "tearings, breakings and dislocations" necessary to attain his spiritual goal, stands in marked contrast to the reluctance of another second-century bishop, Polycarp of Smyrna. He managed to elude the magistrates who were looking for him by hiding in three different houses before he was finally betrayed by a servant, arrested, and executed. Evarestus, Polycarp's biographer, was apparently concerned lest the bishop's flight be construed as weakness. The subsequent *passio* assumed an apologetic tone intent upon presenting a martyrdom "more becoming to the gospel," for Polycarp had "waited to be delivered up, even as the Lord had done." Applauding this combination of sober reluctance and unwavering fortitude, Evarestus posed the case of one Quintus as a counter example. An active seeker of martyrdom of the Ignatius mold, Quintus suffered a last minute flagging of the spirit and apostasized. "Wherefore, brethren, we do not commend those who give themselves up, seeing the gospel does not teach so."[6]

These conflicting patterns of martyrdom which began in the second century begat conflicting theological interpretations in the third. W. H. C. Frend has distinguished between men like Clement of Alexandria, who decried the inherent exhibitionism of the "suicidist and braggart" in search of mindless short cuts to God, and Tertullian, who regarded martyrdom as "something to be invoked, not feared," as the perfect means of imitating Christ.[7] The "rigorism" characteristic of Tertullian's native North Africa would continue to foster radical opinions about martyrdom. The serious threat to Cyprian's episcopal authority in Carthage, following his retreat in the face of the Decian persecutions, was symptomatic of these sentiments.[8] In the fourth century the same attitude would inform the Donatists, for whom willingness to die was regarded as the best recommendation for ecclesiastical office.[9]

Eulogius drew upon the New Testament and the liturgy in his search for precedents. He reminded his readers of Paul's decision to go to Jerusalem despite the visions of the prophet Agabus, which foretold that if Paul went he would be "delivered into the hands of the gentiles" and die.[10] Turning to the passionary, Eulogius recounted in some detail the case of Felix, a student in Mauritania, who, learning of persecutions in Gerona, left for Spain and "triumphantly achieved martyrdom, the opportunity for which was lacking in his own land."[11] Eulogius also listed, without further comment, the names of other "voluntary" martyrs, including Adrian, the Roman officer in Nicomedia who was so impressed by the fortitude of some Christians under torture that he joined them; Eulalia of Barcelona who let nothing, not even her mother's pleading, prevent her from making her Christianity known to the authorities; and Justus and Pastor, two schoolboys who, like Felix, set aside their books to follow what they considered to be the more noble pursuit of their own martyrdom.[12] Their names alone were enough to evoke, in the minds of his readers, the lessons of the passionary that pertained to Eulogius' argument.

Of all the ancient examples that Eulogius garnered, only the story of the seven brothers, which Eulogius knew from the *passio* of St. Julian and St. Basilissa, really served his purpose. According to the passionary account, Diocletian, out of respect for the loyalty of one of his magistrates, allowed his seven sons to practice their Christianity undisturbed. But when the seven brothers witnessed the plight of the Christian Julian in prison, they resolved to join him despite their unique dispensation.[13] When Eulogius' opponents argued that martyrdom made no sense since the Muslims permitted the Christians to practice their religion, this was the most appropriate precedent to which he could appeal.

But even in this case the fit between the ancient and modern martyrs was not as close as Eulogius might have liked. For the Roman confessors, regardless of whether they ran to their deaths or were dragged, died during periods of official persecution. The passionaries underline this point over and over again with such formulaic prefaces as: "In those times, when the demented, sacrilegious fury of the emperors shook the entire world and increased pressure pushed the Christians toward the ungodly cult of the demons..."[14] The picture that these narratives paint is one of an outlawed religion trying to hold its own against an alien government bent on its extirpation. The imperial government, in other words, had created a situation that theoretically forced each Christian to choose between religious compromise and death, thus effectively lifting the responsibility for his or her death from the shoulders of even the most masochistic Christian.

The situation in Muslim Córdoba was quite different. There were no laws against the practice of Christianity nor were any Christians legally bound to demonstrate their loyalty to Muḥammad or Islam. The initiative behind the spontaneous martyrdoms had, therefore, to come from the victims themselves. "No violence on the part of the authorities forced them to deny their faith," and without such provocation the confessors had, in the opinion of their detractors, transgressed the limits of acceptable volition in a way that none of Eulogius' handpicked examples from the passionary could have. Eulogius foresaw this difficulty and did his best to forestall criticism by questioning whether or not the Andalusian church was indeed free from religious persecution. In fact Eulogius would go so far as to demonstrate that the Christians of ninth-century Córdoba were the victims of a persecution at least as pervasive and oppressive as those which plagued the late antique church.

The following passage illustrates one of the ways in which Eulogius attempted to create a sense of Christian persecution:

You do not regard as provocation the destruction of churches, the hate directed towards the priests, and the fact that we pay a monthly tribute with great hardship? Death is more profitable for us than the laborious peril of such a deprived life . . . Who, among all the persecutors of the faithful, has assailed the church as cruelly as this abomination? Who has heaped up so much in subversion of the catholics as this unfortunate one? For no one of us may walk secure in their midst, no one is left in peace, no one may pass through their walls without being dishonored. Whenever the need for any ordinary thing compels us to go forth in public, when it is necessary to go out into the *forum* from our abodes for any household necessity, the moment they notice the symbols of our sacred order, they attack, as if madmen or fools, calling out derision; not to mention the daily mockery of children, for whom it is not enough to inflict verbal abuse and heap up shameful examples of scurrility, but who do not even refrain from pelting us with rocks from behind. Which reminds me of what they do as an insult to the holy sign. For when the psalmody schedule dictates that we give the signal to the faithful, and the approaching hour of prayer obliges us to make the customary indication, these liars, misled by superstition, listen intently to the clang of the reverberating metal and begin to exercise their tongues in every curse and obscenity. Therefore, not unsuitably are they cursed who, with such hate, direct their followers against the clergy. We are calumnied incessantly by them, and everywhere we suffer their ferocity for the sake of religion. Many of them judge us unworthy to touch their garments and curse to themselves if we approach too closely. They deem it pollution if we mix in any of their affairs.[15]

The language and style of this lament over a downtrodden church are reminiscent of those employed by the authors of the Roman *passiones* as they set the stage for their narratives. He could, in fact, have extracted the references to the "laborious peril" and "deprived life" of the Andalusian Christians, as well as the allusions to the ferocity of their enemies, from the mozarabic passionary itself. But, once they are removed from their emotionally charged setting, the specific provocations to which Eulogius alluded fall far short of their Roman counterparts.

The "persecutions" which Eulogius enumerated were: the destruction of churches, taxation, the cursing prompted by the tolling of bells, restricted interpersonal contact between Christians and Muslims, calumny, mockery, rock throwing, and hatred of priests. Keeping in mind the traditional restrictions of the *dhimma* and their sporadic enforcement by the emirs in times of political stress, the provocations that Eulogius delineated were predictable. The recent push to enforce the traditional restrictions on church building could appear persecutory given the laxity with which they were usually applied. Similarly, the hostility that the sound of bells evoked from some Muslims was, whether Eulogius knew it or not, probably a vestige of an old prohibition against bell ringing. The taxes to which Christians were subject were also in accordance with the *dhimma*, though they might well have been increased under ꜥAbd ar-Raḥmān II. Even the type of verbal and physical abuse about which Eulogius complained seems to have been inspired by the spirit behind the pact. For the Christians whom Eulogius described as victims of mockery and pelting were not ordinary Christians, but priests, bearing publicly the "symbol of our sacred order," evoking hostility from those Muslims who regarded their attire as an inappropriately public expression of a subordinate religion.

None of this, of course, mattered to Eulogius. His task was to convince his readers that the Muslims had only one goal in mind as they "weighed down the necks of the faithful with a grievous yoke": "to exclude the entire Christian race . . . from the borders of their kingdom; at times allowing us to exercise Christianity only as it pleases them; other times making our sweat turn foul in servitude to the Pharaonic rite; and still other times imposing a tax on our miserable necks."[16] If this meant exaggerating the ills of Christian life in Córdoba, it was a small price to pay for the vindication of the martyrs.

But this was not the only means that Eulogius employed for creating a sense of persecution. Though Isaac's death was without a doubt the catalyst that led to the first and most virulent outbreak of martyrial dissent, the monk was not, as Eulogius was quick to indicate, the first Christian to suffer at the hands of the Muslim authorities. Prior to Isaac's deliberate flouting of the proscription against blasphemy, Perfectus was arrested and executed for unwittingly committing the same crime. Though this was an entirely unrelated event, Eulogius nevertheless composed an account of the incident, portraying Perfectus as an innocent victim of Muslim faithlessness and false witness, and used it as the opening *passio* of the *Memoriale sanctorum*. Likewise, Eulogius reserved a place in his apology for the merchant Joannes who was not even a martyr, but who had received a harsh punishment for a less flagrant violation of the law against blasphemy.

The cases of Perfectus and Joannes served Eulogius' purposes particularly well in that they helped support his contention that no Christian was safe from victimization at the hands of the Muslims.[17] In fact, on two occasions Eulogius went so far as to suggest that the martyrs' movement as a whole was a direct reaction to the persecutory treatment of Perfectus: "Such a crime, committed against a priest, impelled many, who in the leisure of their secure confession in the lonely mountains were enjoying the solitude of the woods, contemplating God, to come forth to detest and curse, publicly and freely, the sinful prophet."[18] Eulogius wisely made no attempt to account for the fourteen months that separated the execution of Perfectus and Isaac's fateful encounter with the judge.

Perfectus and Joannes were not the only reluctant victims of the Cordoban penal process to find their names incorporated into Eulogius' passionary. Like Perfectus, Argimirus and, most likely, Abundius were arrested for blasphemy and decapitated despite their claims of innocence. In addition, two of the apostates, Aurea and Rudericus, never voluntarily handed themselves over to the authorities. These individual martyrs, it would seem, were not guilty of the charge of excessive volition leveled against the martyrs as a group, for they had not sought their own executions. Eulogius' decision to lump them together with the spontaneous martyrs, like his decision to begin his martyrology with Perfectus and Joannes, should be appreciated in light of his apologetic goal. All of them served as examples of Muslim persecution.

The third and final technique that Eulogius used to create a sense of persecution is best illustrated by his letter to Bishop Wiliesindus of Pamplona, in which he complained of "a fierce, tyrannical madness, rising up against the Church of God," that had "subverted, laid waste, and dispersed everything, dragging bishops, priests, abbots, deacons, and the entire clergy to prison."[19] Again, this passage, with its references to the exercise of tyrannical fury, the subversion and disruption of the church, and the imprisonment of clerics, could have been extracted from the work of some third- or fourth-century hagiographer describing the plight of the church under Decius or Diocletian. Why did Eulogius not refer to these hostile actions on the part of the authorities when listing the precipitating factors behind the martyrs' actions? Because the clerical arrests and imprisonment were not the cause of the martyrdoms, but one of their effects. The "storm" that led to the clerical arrests had gathered in response to the earliest wave of voluntary martyrdoms.

The fact that the arrows of cause and effect pointed in the wrong direction did not deter Eulogius from making the most out of these "persecutions" by focusing on the role they played in encouraging subsequent martyrdoms. Carefully reinterpreting the emirs' actions, Eulogius transformed their basically defensive policy, aimed at preventing any future defamation of the Prophet, into one of aggressive proselytization, a "fierce conspiracy" designed to make Christians "prostrate themselves . . . to their rite."[20]

Despite his efforts to construct a persecutory backdrop for the martyrs' actions, Eulogius characteristically hesitated to lean too heavily on it. Already we have seen him try to vindicate the martyrs by arguing both that there were precedents for spontaneous martyrdom and that the Cordoban Christian community was afflicted with its own persecution. Yet a third approach provided him with a way of transcending the issue altogether by questioning the very criterion that his opponents were applying to his martyrs.

A state of persecution was not, after all, what made a martyr. The definitive element, as Eulogius saw it, was the willingness to bear witness to the truth no matter what the consequences. *Iustitia*, the right order of things, could not tolerate something as aberrant as Christian subjection to a *secta falsa*. From this perspective, the martyrs' unprovoked attacks on Islam made sense, for it was "highly meritorious to subvert the impious, to challenge the enemies of the church, to prepare for war against the adversaries of the faith with the spear of God's word."[21]

Eulogius' use of such "church militant" images has suggested to Allan Cutler that the martyrs were missionaries intent on ushering in the apocalypse through suicidal proselytization. But if we take into consideration Eulogius' habit of leaving no stone unturned in his search for a strong defense, it can be misleading to trust any single motive that he attributed to the martyrs. The single most difficult task that Eulogius faced in his defense of the martyrs was to create a sense of a persecuted community. Having presented as convincing a case as possible for a beleaguered Cordoban church, he stepped back, just as we saw him do in the case of the miracles, and asked rhetorically whether indeed a state of persecution was even necessary to justify the martyrs' actions. If he was to argue successfully that it was not, he had little choice but to refer to Jesus' instructions to his apostles and portray the martyrs as agents of the church militant.

V
The martyrs revisited

9

The martyrs and their motives

Each of the motives that scholars have, over the past four hundred years, attributed to the martyrs of Córdoba can be traced back to some aspect of the literary battle that Eulogius waged on their behalf. The traditional Spanish claim that the martyrs were responding to persecution was simply an extension of Eulogius' argument. French and Dutch scholars opted for the perspective of the unsympathetic Cordoban Christians. Similarly the efforts of Eulogius and Alvarus to recast Islam as the antithesis of Christianity inspired the interpretation of the martyrs as apocalyptically-minded missionaries. Even the "proto-nationalism" thesis, though lacking any direct analogue in the writings of Eulogius, represents little more than a politicization of the polemical line that Eulogius attempted to draw between Muslims and Christians.

We have thus far avoided offering any alternative theories to explain the behavior of the martyrs. From the very beginning, Eulogius has been our primary focus, using his writings to determine who he was, why he wrote in defense of the martyrs, and how he defended their actions. Yet having come to a more thorough understanding of Eulogius, we find ourselves in an advantageous position to comprehend the martyrs. Having a better sense of why Eulogius wrote and what sort of contact he had with the martyrs, we can approach his martyrology more critically and extract the events of the 850s from their apologetic context.

Isaac's behavior in front of the Cordoban judge in the spring of 851 was, as we noted, unprecedented. Though Perfectus had been executed for the same crime some fourteen months before, he had not deliberately flouted the laws against blasphemy. Eulogius was very much aware of this difference in circumstances. As he saw it, Isaac "held the honor of being the *principatus* among the martyrs" of his day because even though Perfectus was killed earlier, "the priest was dragged forcibly to his passion," while the monk went freely to his own.[1] Eulogius' decision to include Perfectus along with four other reluctant martyrs was, we have suggested, a way of strengthening his case on behalf of the martyrs as a whole. In any case, this group of martyrs does not particularly concern us. Our task is to determine what prompted Isaac and others like him to come forward *sponte*, without provocation, to denounce Islam and acclaim the truth of Christianity.

Eulogius, unfortunately, tells us less about Isaac than we would like to know. But what he did record – that Isaac relinquished his position as *exceptor* or *kātib*, entered the monastery at Tabanos, and finally sought a martyr's death – is highly suggestive. While Isaac's reasons for taking each of these steps cannot be ascertained with perfect certainty, we can offer some speculation based on the more complete information we have about other Cordoban Christians who found themselves in similar situations.

The most easily explained step in Isaac's progression from *kātib* to martyr is his choice of the monastery at Tabanos as his retreat. We know from Eulogius' account that Isaac's cousin Hieremia,

famous for his wealth and abounding in material possessions, had, along with his venerable wife Elisabeth, devoted himself sometime before to this *coenobium*, which was built by their families at their own expense, so that he and Elisabeth might dedicate themselves freely for the rest of their lives to the fulfillment of the divine commandments.[2]

But if familial ties account for his choice of Tabanos, they do not help us to understand why he decided to live as a monk in the first place. Fortunately Eulogius was more precise about the paths that led other future martyrs to the monasteries.

Years before Hieremia and Elisabeth retired to Tabanos, they had already taken a step in the direction of withdrawing from the world by vowing to pursue, in their own home, an ascetic lifestyle: *propositum . . . adhuc vulgo admisti gerebant*.[3] By so doing they became, in the language of the church, *poenitentes*.

The role of the penance ritual in the Christian church was to provide the Christian guilty of committing a heinous sin with a way of restoring the spiritual purity of the newly baptized.[4] In its earliest form, as it first appeared in the second century, the process involved a formal petition to the bishop on the part of the sinner for entrance into the order of penitents. For a period of time, which varied according to the flagrancy of the violation, the penitent was excluded from communion and obliged to undertake a spiritually therapeutic regimen of prayer, fasting, and the distribution of alms, and to avoid potentially compromising activities such as sex, business negotiations, and public office.[5] What distinguished this so-called "public" penance from the private type that would begin to supplant it in some areas of continental Europe as early as the ninth century, was not only the duration of the imposed regimen, but the fact that the penance could not be repeated. "Sicut unum baptisma," wrote Ambrose, "ita una poenitentia."[6] The church had nothing but its prayers to offer a relapsed sinner.[7]

Recognizing the great spiritual dangers that the absolved sinner faced, church leaders from early on decided to extend the social restrictions placed on the penitent. Then, even after the prescribed period of penance had elapsed and the penitent was once again allowed to attend mass, sex and the other potentially damning pursuits remained off limits so as to protect the reconciled sinner from a fatal relapse.[8] In the words of R. C. Mortimer, the penitent had become "to all intents and purposes a professed religious."[9]

As onerous as the *ordo poenitentiae* must have appeared to Christians obliged to enter it in expiation of a mortal sin, it proved a strong magnet for others who, while not guilty of any particular infraction, were attracted to the ascetic discipline that it involved. The late antique church had to cater to the needs of a growing number of Christians who voluntarily adopted the religious regimen and social liabilities associated with public penance.[10]

The popularity of this *poenitantia spontanea* among lay men and women seems itself to have been a product of the inherent limitations of a penitential system based on *poenitentia coactitia*. Because each Christian could apply for the cleansing effects of public penance only once in a lifetime, it became a standard practice to postpone penance until the deathbed to minimize the occasion for relapse.[11] While this may have proved the safest avenue in terms of the ultimate goal of salvation, such procrastination afforded little in the way of solace for anyone anxious about a lifelong accumulation of venial sins. Voluntary penance offered the conscientious Christian not only a way of avoiding many potentially sinful situations, but an opportunity to make a positive contribution to his or her own spiritual standing by means of a self-imposed ascetic discipline.[12]

The frequency of references in church councils, especially those of Visigothic Spain, to Christians who "received penance without having confessed any palpable sins" attests to the increasing popularity of this religious option in the century before the Muslim invasion.[13] The terms used to describe the penitents in the conciliar canons varied according to the circumstances of their profession, as well as their gender and marital status. The ecclesiastics who attended the fourth council of Toledo distinguished first of all between those who received penance voluntarily and those who, in their minority, were dedicated by their parents. The same canon divided the female penitents into three groups: virgins, widows, and married *poenitentibus feminis*.[14] In each case the *professio poenitentiae* entailed the donning of a "religious habit" in church or in the presence of a priest, an act which symbolized the individual's decision to renounce worldly attachments. The ease with which a layperson could adopt a life of penance stood in marked contrast to the subsequent difficulty of resuming a normal secular life. Like monks, penitents were permanently bound to their professions. Predictably, the majority of the canons related to such penitents were aimed at preventing those who had assumed the *habitum religiosum* from later reverting to the *habitum laicalem*. To this end the councils repeatedly authorized bishops and priests to enforce the penitent's commitment with threats of anathema.[15]

It is interesting, in light of what we know about Hieremia's and Elisabeth's decision to retire to Tabanos, that the councils also made a distinction between those penitents who chose to lead their socially restricted lives at home and those who retired to monasteries.[16] The domestic option did not lend itself to effective ecclesiastical control, a situation that provoked commentary from more than one Visigothic churchman. Leander of Seville, the older brother of Isidore, once wrote to his sister, asking her to "flee the private life" that always "constricts with a multitude of concerns the lives of the virgins who remain in cells in the cities." He advised her instead to live *regulariter* like the monks in a monastery.[17]

We do not know whether the decision of Hieremia and Elisabeth to transplant their domestic regimen to the mountains of Tabanos was prompted by their own conscience or by the urgings of a concerned ecclesiastic. But regardless of the circumstances, the monastery at Tabanos seems to have served their spiritual needs as a family-owned and operated retreat inhabited by penitents like themselves seeking the most conducive environment for the fulfillment of their individual *proposita*.[18]

This type of familial monastery was a very common feature of early medieval Europe in general,[19] and the canons of the Toledan councils attest to the frequency of such arrangements in Visigothic Spain. Rich laymen who built churches and monasteries on their own land could retain a great deal of control over the maintenance of the church fabric, the collection of revenues, and the appointment of the priests, abbots, and other appropriate clerics.[20] Such provisions were intended to protect these privately sponsored institutions from any excessive encroachment of episcopal jurisdiction, especially in the form of revenue tapping.[21] Of course such extensive lay powers led to various abuses of their own. Fructuosus, who dedicated much of his literary energies to the composition of rules that would help to regulate the reception of families into religious life, once observed that:

> Some are accustomed out of fear of hell to establish monasteries for themselves in their homes, and with their wives, children, servants, and neighbors, to join themselves together by means of the terms of an oath, and in their own *villae*, as we have said, to consecrate churches in the name of the martyrs, and call them, falsely, monasteries. We, however, do not consider them to be monasteries, but rather see them as the perdition of souls and the subversion of the church.[22]

Fructuosus was not against the establishment of family monasteries *per se*. He was suspicious of those which lacked control, those in which the inhabitants lived "according to their own will, not wanting to be subject to any superiors."[23] He would presumably not have objected to the situation at Tabanos where the female and male inhabitants were separated by a wall, subject to Elisabeth and her brother Martinus respectively.

There is no indication that Isaac lived as a penitent in his own home prior to entering the monastery. Given the fact that by 848, when he relinquished his office and decided to live the life of a religious, the family retreat at Tabanos was already well-established, there would have been little reason for Isaac to consider any other option. Nevertheless, the new life that Isaac assumed at

Tabanos was, like that of his cousin, one which allowed him to live out a *sanctum propositum*.[24]

If we keep this relationship between voluntary penance and Cordoban monasticism in mind, we will be in a much better position to understand Isaac's ultimate confrontation with the judge. For in fact the step from monk to martyr was, unlike that from *kātib* to monk, less qualitative than quantitative, representing more than anything else a heightening of the spiritual anxieties that had pushed him to the monastery in the first place. Martyrdom was in fact a perfect solution to the spiritual anxiety produced by an inflexible penitential system. Not only did it epitomize self-abnegation and separation from the world, but it guaranteed that there would be no opportunity to sin again. It represented a uniquely inviolable stage of penitential discipline. Again, the limited information that we have about Isaac makes it difficult to confirm this connection between his martyrdom and the *propositum* that he observed at Tabanos. But we can extrapolate from the cases of some of the other martyrs.

Columba was impressed by her sister Elisabeth's decision to lead a life of domestic penance. "Frequently visiting her sister at her home," Eulogius wrote, Columba "longed to consign herself to the same sort of vows and desired to become a zealous servant of the same *propositum*."[25] But this did not fit into her mother's plan to give her remaining daughter away in marriage. As it happened, however, Columba's mother died before she could realize her intentions. By then, Elisabeth had left for Tabanos with her husband Hieremia and her brother Martinus, and Columba hastened to join them.

Eulogius' account of Columba's experience at Tabanos is, despite its hyperbole, revealing. Columba suffered from overwhelming anxiety about her own spritual shortcomings, a profound uncertainty about her own ability to resist temptation. "She was thus encouraged to pursue greater sanctity, and, driven by her fear of the enemy, she struggled for the height of virtue in the midst of a harassed life. The tempter frequently tormented her with anxieties, incited pride, simulated the form of men, added food, and wore her down with various dreams. Shaken with fear of these things, she mourned excessively lest she be deprived upon death of the company of [Christ,] her spouse."[26]

Presumably Columba's decision to follow her siblings to Tabanos was the first step toward alleviating these anxieties. But could she even count on the discipline of the monastic life to relieve her stress? The fact that, as Eulogius reports, she ultimately chose to separate herself from her sisters and engage in more than the normal share of austerities suggests that she was not certain. And this uncertainty made the prospect of martyrdom attractive to her:

Unceasingly engaged in these devotions, and pursuing the burden of her vigils, fasts and prayers, holy Columba inflicted upon herself more punishment, I reckon, than any executioner could have. Yet it was as if all the torment she brought upon herself was nothing; as if she had no confidence in her own merits, though she undertook great things. Afraid lest the hundredth fruit of her virginity appear empty of merit in the eyes of the father, she aspired toward the ineffable wealth of martyrdom, which sends the sinner on a direct path to the kingdom of heaven.[27]

Chastity, the keystone of the penitential regimen, was not enough for Columba. Avoiding evil was not, in her eyes, as meritorious as actively seeking after the good. Martyrdom presented her with an opportunity to contribute in a positive way toward her own salvation.

Columba was not the only confessor who demonstrated an intense preoccupation with her spiritual status and serious doubts about her ability to achieve the desired level of purity through the established channels. Eulogius' account of the events leading up to the deaths of Sabigotho and her husband Aurelius reveals the same sort of religious intensity.

Sabigotho and Aurelius married as secret apostates and were content to practice their Christianity clandestinely for a number of years. Aurelius was, however, more comfortable with this situation than Sabigotho:

While I was living for myself, dead to God, you, my sweet wife, with unremitting exhortation, always tried to lead me to confession, pressuring me daily to separate myself from the pleasures of the world. You placed the happiness of the eternal kingdom above the dark affections of the world. You attempted to persuade me to relinquish all sin. You spoke highly of the monks and praised those who had renounced the world, delighting in the conversation of the religious, frequently sighing over the lives of the saints. But I, not yet illuminated with the compunction of celestial grace, was by no means able to acquiesce to your salutary exhortations. Or perchance, not yet following the admonition prescribed by God the father for my correction, I put off pursuing that which I envisioned, albeit tenuously, in my mind.[28]

The turning point for Aurelius came in early 851 when he witnessed the beating of Joannes. He recalled to Eulogius how he had heard the crowd clamoring for the merchant's execution, and how the serenity with which the Christian withstood the lashes and the humiliation inspired him to tend to the state of his own soul. Returning home he expressed his intentions to his wife:

Behold, my dearest one, the time has come. The days of our salvation are at hand, in which, recoiling from external and past things, we project ourselves into that which lies ahead of us. First of all, striving perfectly for purity and continence, let us take time for prayer, by means of which we may hasten more easily to the holy work that remains. May you, who were my wife, now become my sister; let the bed of our union give way to fraternal affection. Let offspring of the spirit emerge from it, let a generation of the spirit grow out of it. Having disdained the filth of such bodily union, the mind, free from carnal desire, will learn to produce progeny in the form of eternal salvation.[29]

The road that Aurelius had finally decided to follow was the same as that taken by Hieremia and Elisabeth: that of domestic penance. As Eulogius reported, he and his wife slept in separate beds, wore hair shirts, fasted, prayed, and tended to the needs of the imprisoned Christians.[30]

As in the case of Columba, Sabigotho's regimen did not entirely satisfy her. Her frequent visits to the cell of Flora and Maria made her all the more cognizant of the incomparable quality of their mode of self-denial. Once the two had been executed, Sabigotho was left alone with her concerns, more anxious than ever about her ability to achieve her goal through voluntary penance. In this state of mind she experienced a vision in which Flora and Maria approached her resplendent in their celestial glory. Sabigotho quickly availed herself of this opportunity to obtain some reassurance:

Tell me if I shall receive the benefits of my vows, lest running to no end, I perish into nothingness; lest my efforts turn out to be in vain; lest, while my whole intention seeks one thing, my merit aims at another. Because God favors merit more than prayers, he is known to have rejected a multitude of prayers that is not aided by any dignity of merit. Therefore my lords, wives of Christ, tell me if up until now my hope of sustaining the reward of your spouse has stood on firm ground.

One could hardly ask for a more direct and succinct statement of the type of spiritual uneasiness that characterized those confessors about whom we have any detailed information. Sabigotho, a woman who voluntarily assumed the *habitum religiosum* of penance and had thus irrevocably devoted the rest of her life to continence, prayer, and acts of charity, was nonetheless frightened lest, for some lack of merit, her dreams be thwarted. The response that she received from the virgins comforted her, but did not really answer her question:

The profits of your labor are deposited in heaven and are preserved for you to collect at the right time. Nor will the things necessary for battle, which compel the invincible athletes to go forth to the kingdom, be lacking. For martyrdom has been predestined and fixed for you from the time the world was created.[31]

Yes, the types of austerities associated with the penitential lifestyle have value, but do they have enough to insure salvation? In Sabigotho's case the point was moot. She was destined to experience the ultimate act of self-denial, one which would far outshine her previous efforts.

Though the majority of the *passiones* are not nearly as detailed as those we have just considered, we can tell by association or by the use of certain characteristic terms that Columba, Aurelius, and Sabigotho were not isolated cases. We know, for example, little about Felix and Liliosa except that they were guilty of apostasy, that Felix was related to Aurelius, and that the couple's fate was bound up with that of Aurelius and Sabigotho. Yet we can be fairly certain that they followed the other couple's example and lived as domestic penitents prior to handing themselves over to martyrdom. In the case of Fandila, Eulogius wrote only that, out of fear of God, "he dictated his mind to heaven, despising all earthly things, and longed more to be killed and thus be with Christ, than to remain bound to filth."[32] But the fact that his formative years prior to becoming a priest at the monastery at San Salvador were spent under the *regulari disciplina vel regimine* of abbot Martinus at Tabanos speaks for itself. The austerities in which Flora engaged prior to her martyrdom were part of her effort to "fulfill her vow as a wife of Christ."[33] Finally, we know that when Maria's mother died, not only did her father "set out on the narrow path of eternal life," having aspired to the *gradu confessionis*, but he made certain that his son Walabonsus would be raised *ecclesiasticis regulis*, and dedicated his daughter as a virgin to God.[34]

We find evidence of this spiritual anxiety not only in the *passiones* but in the apologetic portions of Eulogius' martyrologies. At one point the priest attributed the spontaneity of the martyrs' confessions to their search "for a short cut by which, freed from their bodies, they might come more quickly to their celestial homeland."[35] Elsewhere, in defense of the absence of miracles, Eulogius pointed out that the intention of the martyrs was not to perform signs but to inscribe their names in heaven.[36] Interestingly enough, the detractors themselves were aware of the personal spiritual motives that lay behind the martyrdoms. They accused the confessors of selfishness, being more concerned about their own salvation than about the fate of the Andalusian Christian community as a whole. Such audaciously suicidal behavior, in their opinion, was motivated by pride, *initium omnis peccati*. It proved that the confessors were "indiscreet and unwilling to suffer with the weaker Christians, striving instead to purchase the comfort of their own peace and tranquility in heaven with their blood."[37]

It is also significant that in one of the later Arabic accounts of a Cordoban Christian seeking martyrdom, the author presents the Christian as an ill-informed fanatic with his eye on a quick and easy way to an assured salvation. When the *qāḍī* Aslam ibn ʿAbd al-ʿAzīz asked the Christian why he would want to die when he had committed no crime, the Christian responded that only his corporeal self would die, while his true self would immediately ascend to heaven.[38]

There is, then, evidence, both direct and indirect, for attributing at least some of the martyrdoms to acute spiritual anxiety on the part of the confessors. This is, in fact, the only explanation with any kind of a textual basis apart from the polemics and apologetics that surrounded the executions. But the picture is still not complete. If indeed this type of penitential *angst* were the key ingredient in the recipe for a martyrs' movement, would we be safe in assuming that it was, in itself, sufficient to cause the martyrdoms? Was the spiritual stress to which Cordoban Christians were susceptible any more intense than that which afflicted Christians in other parts of Europe?

The decision to lead a penitential or monastic life, by definition, involved a critique of one's previous existence, a rejection of the secular world within which one had hitherto operated. This was true of *poenitentes* and monks in Christian Europe as well as those who lived in Muslim Spain. But in the latter case, the fact that the surrounding secular society was at least theoretically Islamic added a new dimension to this critique. A rejection of the world became indistinguishable from a rejection of Islam. Under these special circumstances, a decision to abandon the world was easily transformed into a statement of religious identity. This may explain why the confessors ultimately chose the particular means of invoking their martyrdom that they did: a public denunciation of Islam and profession of faith in Christianity. It also suggests that those Christians who remained a part of Andalusian society might have suffered from a certain defensiveness about their own religious identities, which the example of the monks would only have exacerbated.

Though the identification of Islam and the secular world may have contributed to the negative sentiments that the *poenitentes* and monks felt toward Islam, it does not really explain what prompted them to take as radical a step as martyrdom. This brings us to a second major point. It is not enough to show that the spontaneous martyrdoms were a response to obsessive concerns about personal salvation and the need to reject an Islamic world. If this were all that there was to it then why do we not see any unprovoked martyrdoms before 851, when presumably the spiritual concerns of Cordoban Christians were much the same?

The answer is simply that no one before Isaac had ever conceived of spontaneous martyrdom as an option. There was, prior to Isaac's dramatic gesture, no precedent for behavior of this sort. As we saw in the previous two chapters, the circumstances in al-Andalus did not suggest obvious parallels to the situation in imperial Rome, where martyrdom was an accepted Christian response. The Andalusian Christians were not subject to pagan rule nor were they the target of any organized persecution. When, however, Isaac publicly asserted the exclusive truth of Christianity and the falsehood of Islam, he provided a new perspective, one which emphasized the similarities between ninth-century al-Andalus and third-century Rome. And his subsequent martyrdom, which made perfect sense in light of the antithetical relationship that he attributed to Christianity and Islam, opened the door to waves of imitators, many of whom recognized the act of martyrdom as the perfect realization and culmination of their penitential programs.[39]

This brings us back to our original question: what was it that prompted Isaac to take the unprecedented step from monk to spontaneous martyr? The answer perhaps lies in the unusual circumstances that surrounded his retirement. The best clue we have as to why Isaac gave up his government position is the manner in which he invoked his martyrdom. As we have already seen, Isaac approached the judge asking for instruction in the tenets of Islam, as if he were considering conversion. Only after the official expounded at length on various doctrinal points did Isaac make his true intentions clear, railing against the poor judgement of a man who, despite his scholarly achievements, was incapable of recognizing the errors of Islam. None of the subsequent confessors ever made a similar request of a Muslim official. With few exceptions they launched directly into their diatribes against Islam.

It is difficult to make sense of the judge's willingness to cooperate with Isaac and his utter shock when the monk insulted him if he did not have reason to believe that his explanation would indeed have a positive effect, to wit, the monk's conversion. Now we know that one of Isaac's successors as *exceptor* fell victim to Muḥammad I's purge of the Cordoban bureaucracy some months after the new emir took power. We also know that a short time later the same official converted to Islam and was reinstated. It is possible, given the perennial nature of *dhimmī* purges of this sort in other parts of the Muslim world,[40] that Isaac too had lost his position as a result of his religious affiliation. If that was indeed the case, then the Muslim judge from whom he solicited information about Islam, a man who probably knew Isaac from his years of employment in the palace, would have regarded Isaac's request as a logical first step toward resuming his duties as *kātib*.

If Isaac's official position did become contingent upon his conversion to Islam, his resignation may have marked the first time in his life that he had defined himself religiously. Given the general tendency of Andalusian Christians to maintain a low religious profile in the interests of assimilating into Islamic society, the climate was right for cases of second conversion. The voluntary assumption of penitential discipline, a decisive phase in many of the confessors' lives, was one particularly popular way of demonstrating a renewed commitment to Christianity, of publicly defining oneself as a Christian. In Isaac's case the precipitating factor – the threat of dismissal from his post as *kātib* – forced him to weigh his position against his religious identity, to decide whether or not his Christianity was expendable. The change in religiosity from a Christian bureaucrat who must have espoused the most "ecumenical" attitudes towards the Muslims to have risen as high as he did in government service, to a monk who would have quite naturally equated Andalusian Islamic society with the world that he had rejected, was a radical one. It may even have been radical enough to prompt him to demonstrate his repudiation of Islam and identification with Christianity with a singularly dramatic gesture.[41]

The combination of spiritually insecure Christians and a spontaneous martyr was a volatile one. Neither ingredient in isolation could have produced anything like the Cordoban martyrs' movement. Had Isaac stayed in Tabanos instead of confronting the Muslim judge, Hieremia, Columba, Aurelius, and Sabigotho would presumably have lived out their lives as penitents or monks, engaging in all of the usual austerities in their search for a sense of spiritual security. And had there not been Christians such as these, who were ready to try anything to relieve the fear that all of their efforts at securing their salvation might be in vain, Isaac would have been an isolated victim of the Islamic proscriptions against blasphemy.

Notes

1 Christians in Muslim Córdoba

1 Antonio Arjona Castro, *Anales de Córdoba musulmana* (Córdoba, 1983), pp. 13–14. For a variation of the account, see: Ahmed ibn Mohammed al-Makkari, *The History of the Mohammedan Dynasties in Spain*, tr. Pascual de Gayangos, 2 vols. (London, 1840), 1:277–80.

2 This was a common practice in Spain at the time of the conquest, as Eliyahu Ashtor, in his *The Jews of Moslem Spain* (Philadelphia, 1973), pp. 15–26, indicates. Arabic chroniclers report the establishment of similar Jewish garrisons in Granada, Toledo, and Seville (al-Makkari 1:280, 282, 284), and claim that the practice "became the fixed method of the conquerors" (Ashtor, p. 24). Most historians agree that the harsh treatment of the Jews under Visigothic rule, as evidenced by the Toledan councils of the seventh century, led the Jews to applaud the change of leadership. José Vives, ed., *Concilios visigóticos e hispano-romanos* (Barcelona, 1963), e.g., Toledo 4.57–66 (633), pp. 210–14, and Toledo 17.8 (694), pp. 534–6.

3 This Christian leader was, according to Arabic sources, the only "prince" captured during the conquest. All of the others either capitulated or fled with greater success. al-Makkari 2:15.

4 Some Arab sources indicate that the first mosque in Damascus was also part of a church, but other evidence suggests this was not the case. A. S. Tritton, *The Caliphs and their Non-Muslim Subjects: A Critical Study of the Covenant of ᶜUmar* (London, 1930), pp. 9–10, 39, 40–2.

5 Al-Makkari 1:217.

6 *The Holy Qur'an*, trans., A. Yusuf Ali, 2nd ed., 1977, Sūra 9.29, p. 447; S.2.62, pp. 33–4. Cf., S.5.69, p. 265.

7 Thomas F. Glick, *Islamic and Christian Spain in the Early Middle Ages* (Princeton, 1979), p. 169. Many historians have marveled at this "tolerance." But, as Glick (p. 174) has observed, "The communal autonomy of the groups, often represented as the very symbol of tolerance, was in fact the institutional expression of ethnocentric norms which held such groups in abhorrence, as tolerated but alienated citizens who were not to share in social life on the same basis as members of the dominant religion." Robert I. Burns, S.J., noted the same phenomenon in thirteenth-century Valencia, where the political tables had been turned and the Christians were segregating themselves from the Muslim majority: "Tolerance at this extreme is not easily distinguishable from intolerance." *Islam under the Crusaders* (Princeton, 1973), pp. 186–7.

8 Majid Khadduri, *War and Peace in the Law of Islam* (Baltimore, 1955), p. 178.

Antoine Fattal, *Le statut légal des non-musulmans en pays d'Islam* (Beirut, 1958), p. 21.

9 Khadduri, p. 179.

10 Francisco X. Simonet, *Historia de los mozárabes de España* (Madrid, 1903), pp. 797–8. Although this is the only capitulation agreement that has survived from the peninsular conquest, others are mentioned by Arab historians. The heirs of Witiza and Roderick, the two Visigothic pretenders to the throne, both retained their rights to family property in exchange for their cooperation. Al-Makkari 2:14, 30. See also: Alfred M. Howell, "Some Notes on Early Treaties Between Muslims and the Visigothic Rulers of Al-Andalus," in *Actas del I Congreso de historia de Andalucía*, diciembre de 1976, Andalucía medieval, v. 1 (Córdoba, 1978), pp. 3–14.

11 A *dhimmī* is someone bound by the constraints of a *dhimma*, in the case of Spain, a Christian or a Jew living under Muslim rule. The conquerors did not typically extend the protection of property to those Christians who either resisted or fled. We know in the case of Mérida that the conquerors confiscated the property of all those who either died in combat or fled to Galicia. Simonet, p. 52.

12 The only exceptions during the initial phase of Islamic expansion were Ctesiphon, where morale problems prompted the change in policy in the first place, and cities in Syria where pre-existing treaties governed settlement patterns. Marshall G. S. Hodgson, *The Venture of Islam*, 3 vols. (New York, 1972), 1:208.

13 It is difficult to determine whether or not the lack of a garrison in Córdoba was typical of the Iberian conquest as a whole. Roger Collins apparently assumes that the use of separate garrisons was as characteristic of Spain as it was of other areas conquered, but he does not devote any detailed attention to the problem. *Early Medieval Spain: Unity and Diversity, 400–1000* (New York, 1983), p. 160. In any case it is interesting to note that when regional resistance to Cordoban authority began to proliferate in the next century, the emirs typically ordered the erection of garrisons in the most strategic areas of the troubled provinces. Such was the case in Zaragoza in 802, Mérida in 834, and Calatrava in 853. Evariste Lévi-Provençal, *Histoire de l'Espagne musulmane*, 3 vols., 2nd ed. (Paris, 1950), 1:156, 209, 292.

14 Tritton, p. 43. ʿUmar II and al-Mutawakkil (847–61) were the two most significant reformers of this type. Both sought to restrict *dhimmī* activity during times of particular political stress. Bernard Lewis, *The Jews of Islam* (Princeton, 1984), pp. 46–9.

15 Norman A. Stillman, *The Jews of Arab Lands* (Philadelphia, 1979), p. 157.

16 Tritton, p. 104; Stillman, p. 158.

17 Tritton, p. 116.

18 Tritton, p. 117.

19 Stillman, pp. 157–8.

20 Lewis, p. 27.

21 Pierre Guichard, *Al-Andalus: estructura antropológica de una sociedad islámica en occidente* (Barcelona, 1970), p. 81.

22 Glick, pp. 33–5.

23 Severus, *History of the Patriarchs of the Coptic Church of Alexandria*, ed. R. Graffin and F. Nau, *Patrologia Orientalis*, vols. 1, 5, 6, 10 (Paris, 1907–15).

24 *Memoriale sanctorum* 1.21 (PL 115:754; CSM 2:385); Eulogius, *Documentum martyriale* 18 (PL 115:830; CSM 2:470).

25 Paulus Alvarus, *Indiculus luminosus* 3 (PL 121:518; CSM 1:275).

26 The exact amount of taxation seems to have always been left to the discretion of the individual emir. The *Chronica muzarabica*, a mid-eighth-century continuation of Isidore's *Chronicon*, is full of references to changes in the levels of *dhimmī* taxation. As early as the 720s the Christians were complaining of the *vectigalia duplicata* imposed by the governor ʿAnbasa. As soon as he was replaced by Yaḥya ibn Salama, however, the money was restored to the Christians. *Chronica muzarabica* 60–1 (CSM 1:39). The references in the writings of Eulogius and Alvarus could have reflected the general increase of taxes under the emir ʿAbd ar-Raḥmān II that we know about from independent sources: the historian Ibn Saʿīd and Louis the Pious who, in 826, sent a letter to the people of Mérida hoping to secure an alliance against the emir. Al-Makkari 1:124. MGH *Epistolarum* 5.1, ed. Karl Hampe (Berlin, 1898), p. 115.

27 *Memoriale sanctorum* 2.1 (PL 115:766; CSM 2:398). *Indiculus luminosus* 3 (PL 121:518; CSM 1:276).

28 *Memoriale sanctorum* 1.9 (PL 115:746–7; CSM 2:377–8); *Indiculus luminosus* 5 (PL 121:520; CSM 1:277–8). It is significant that Saʿīd ibn Sulaiman, the *qāḍī*, or judge, at the time of Perfectus' death and John's punishment, was appointed in the latter part of ʿAbd ar-Raḥmān II's reign (822–52), after the emir had removed his predecessor from the same office for excessive lenience in the sentencing of a Muslim blasphemer. This precedent no doubt influenced Saʿīd's treatment of the two arrested Christians. *Historia de los jueces*, pp. 127–9.

29 *Indiculus luminosus* 6 (PL 121:521; CSM 1:278–9).

30 *Indiculus luminosis* 6 (PL 121:521; CSM 1:278). Eulogius, *Liber apologeticus martyrum* 33 (PL 115:867; CSM 2:493).

31 Eulogius, *Memoriale sanctorum* 1.21 (PL 115:755: CSM 2:386).

32 *Indiculus luminosus* 6 (PL 121:521; CSM 1:278).

33 *Memoriale sanctorum* 1.21 (PL 115:754; CSM 2:385).

34 CSM 2:668.

35 The only mention by an Arab chronicler of any special clothing worn by the *dhimmī*s in al-Andalus is a reference to yellow as being a color reserved for the woolen caps worn by Jews. Al-Makkari 1:116. The only reference to a *zunnār* being worn by Cordoban Christians is an eleventh-century description of clerical garb. Al-Makkari 1:246. Moreover, by the ninth century, the effects of intermarriage had begun contributing to the physical homogenization of the population.

36 The monasteries located in the nearby mountain villages of Tabanos and Pinna Mellaria were both recently established as family retreats. *Memoriale sanctorum* 2.2 (PL 115:770; CSM 2:402), 3.11.2 (PL 115:812; CSM 2:453).

37 These include the monasteries at Tabanos and Pinna Mellaria, along with St. Martin's at Rojana and the monastery of St. Justus and St. Pastor at Fraga. Another, dedicated to St. Zoilus, was located still further north behind the Sierra Morena.

38 The monastery of St. Christopher lay just downriver within sight of the city, while those dedicated to the Virgin and to St. Felix were located further southwest in the village of Cuteclara.

39 The ones that he mentions are the *basilicae* of St. Acisclus, St. Zoilus, St. Cyprian, and St. Faustus, St. Januarius, and St. Martialis.

40 Al-Makkari 1:246. A Cordoban calendar, dating from 961, includes references to some of the same monasteries and churches, as well as many that Eulogius never mentioned. Reinhart P. A. Dozy, *Le Calendrier de Cordoue*, 2nd ed., trans.

C. Pellat, Medieval Iberian Peninsula Texts and Studies, vol. 1 (Leyden, 1961).

41 Alvarus, *Vita Eulogii* 2.4 (PL 115:709; CSM 1:332). Reccafredus may have been the metropolitan of Seville. Though he attended a council in 839 as the bishop of Córdoba and Cabra (CSM: 1:141), Saul served as bishop of Córdoba during the martyrdoms. See: Colbert, p. 176.

42 Lévi-Provençal 1:164.

43 Ibid, 1:196.

44 Ibn Khaldun (d. 1406), in his description of the duties of the *khaṭṭāt ash-ashghal*, or tax collector, indicated that it was customary under the ʿUmayyads to appoint liberated slaves or members of an *ahl adh-dhimma* (people of the covenant). Al-Makkari 1, app. B, p. xxxi. Samson, who became abbot of Pinna Mellaria in 858, composed his *Apologeticus* in response to what he regarded as reprehensible conduct on the parts of count Servandus of Córdoba and bishop Hostegesis of Málaga, who had both engaged, among other things, in tax collecting. *Apologeticus* 2 pref., 5 (CSM 2:551). Eulogius also railed vehemently against Christian tax farmers who "crucified Christ's members daily." *Memoriale sanctorum* 3.5 (PL 115:803; CSM 2:443). Sanctius, one of the first of the spontaneous martyrs, was a soldier in the emir's service, and the fact that one of Muḥammad I's strategies for stemming the flow of martyrs was to reduce military pensions suggests that Sancho was not alone. *Memoriale sanctorum* 2.3 (PL 115:771; CSM 2:402), 3.1 (PL 115:800; CSM 2:440).

45 *Apologeticus* 2 pref., 9 (CSM 2:554).

46 *Memoriale sanctorum* 3.16 (PL 115:815; CSM 2:455-6).

47 Eulogius, *Epistula* 3.8 (PL 115:848; CSM 2:500).

48 *Memoriale sanctorum* 2.2 (PL 115:770; CSM 2:402).

49 *Historia de los jueces de Córdoba por Aljoxani*, trans. Julián Ribera (Madrid, 1914), pp. 159-64. *Historia de la conquista de España por Abenalcotía*, trans. Julián Ribera (Madrid, 1926), pp. 67-9. *Memoriale sanctorum* 2.15.2 (PL 115:796; CSM 2:435), 3.2 (PL 115:801; CSM 2:440).

50 Al-Makkari 1:103.

51 *Memoriale sanctorum* 2.15.2 (PL 115:796; CSM 2:435).

52 *Memoriale sanctorum* 1, pref., 3 (PL 115:738; CSM 2:368).

53 *Memoriale sanctorum* 2.1.6 (PL 115:770; CSM 2:401).

54 Lévi-Provençal 1:163.

55 Ibid., 1:166-8.

56 Eulogius, *Epistula* 3.10 (PL 115:849; CSM 2:501); *Vita Eulogii* 2.4 (PL 115:709; CSM 1:332). It is uncertain how many of the Cordoban clerics were victims of this detention, but we can safely assume, given the point of the arrests, that at least the most prominent ones were involved. Whether or not it was Reccafredus who came up with the idea in the first place, he was the one pinpointed by Alvarus as the culprit.

57 *Memoriale sanctorum* 2.15.3 (PL 115:796; CSM 2:435).

58 *Memoriale sanctorum* 2.16.2 (PL 115:797; CSM 2:436), 3.1 (PL 115:800-1; CSM 2:439). Ecclesiasticus 10.2.

59 *Memoriale sanctorum* 3.2 (PL 115:801; CSM 2:440-1).

60 Most recently, see James Waltz, "The significance of the voluntary martyrs' movement of ninth-century Córdoba," *Muslim World* 60 (1970), pp. 152-3.

61 *Memoriale sanctorum* 3.1 (PL 115:801; CSM 2:440).

62 For background on the Malikite school in Spain, see, in particular, Hussain Mones, "Le rôle des hommes de religion dans l'histoire de l'Espagne

musulmane jusqu'à la fin du califat," *Studia Islamica* 20 (1964), pp. 47–88, and Abdel Magid Turki, "La vénération pour Mālik et la physionomie de malikisme andalou," *Studia Islamica* 33 (1971), 41–65.

63 *Memoriale sanctorum* 3.4 (PL 115:802; CSM 2:441).

64 The fact that the Christian kingdoms of northern Spain were asserting themselves politically at the expense of the Cordoban emirate only served to make the Muslim rulers more suspicious of Christian dissent in their own backyard. The Andalusian Jews, on the other hand, had "no secret relationships with factors outside the government that might frighten the Moslem rulers of the peninsula." Ashtor, p. 56.

65 Lévi-Provençal was very much aware of the political nature of the crackdown on the Cordoban Christian community: "If the reigns of many ʿUmayyad emirs were marked by persecutions of Christian communities, of that of Córdoba in particular, . . . one must recognize that these persecutions were dictated less by the fanaticism of the princes than by their political preoccupations." Lévi-Provençal, p. 226. This was an opinion inherited from Reinhart P. A. Dozy, *Histoire des musulmans d'Espagne jusqu'à la conquête de l'Andalousie par les almoravides*, 3 vols., rev. Lévi-Provençal (Leiden, 1932), 1:338.

66 *Memoriale sanctorum* 3.3 (PL 115:801–2; CSM 2:441). Eulogius expressed his outrage, not so much at the emir's order, as at its execution. For in the process, "the prince of darkness also tore down temples that had been erected . . . 300 years ago." This reference to pre-conquest churches in Córdoba does not fit ar-Rāzī's account very well. Perhaps the Arab historian was referring to a specific radius around Córdoba, outside of which the original conquerors ignored the churches.

67 *Memoriale sanctorum* 3.4 (PL 115:802; CSM 2:441). The only known casualty was the monastery at Tabanos, which was destroyed sometime during the summer of 853 between the martyrdoms of Digna (June 14) and Columba (September 17). *Memoriale sanctorum* 3.8.2 (PL 115:805; CSM 2:445), 3.10.9 (PL 115:809–10; CSM 2:450). The tenth-century calendar of Córdoba lists some of the familiar churches and monasteries of the previous century as sites of saint day celebrations. Dozy, *Le Calendrier*.

68 Al-Ḥakam I had resorted to the establishment of a garrison at Calatrava to deal with the Toledans. Al-Makkari 2:428, note 25.

69 Guichard, p. 278.

70 Al-Makkari 2:127. Lévi-Provençal 1:293–4.

71 Guichard, pp. 274–5, 278.

72 Eulogius regarded the new series of anti-Christian measures in 857 as a direct result of peace in the provinces. *Liber apologeticus martyrum* 22 (PL 115:863; CSM 2:488–9).

73 *Memoriale sanctorum* 3.7.4 (PL 115:805; CSM 2:445). According to Eulogius, Muḥammad's predecessor had at one point considered the same course of action. Ibid., 2.12 (PL 115:793; CSM 2:432). These were not necessarily exaggerations on Eulogius' part, nor idle threats on the part of the emirs. Al-Ḥakam I, as we have seen, dealt with the revolt of 818 by razing the rebellious quarter and deporting its inhabitants.

2 The martyrs of Córdoba

1 *Memoriale sanctorum* 2.2 (PL 115:770; CSM 2:402).
2 *Memoriale sanctorum* 1, pref., 2 (PL 115:736–7; CSM 2:367).
3 *Memoriale sanctorum* 1, pref., 2–3 (PL 115:737; CSM 2:367–8).
4 *Memoriale sanctorum* 1, pref., 2–3 (PL 115:736–7; CSM 2:367–8). This type of crucifixion was a common penalty for treason and other serious offenses in the Islamic world. Eulogius uses the terms *stipes*, *eculeus*, and *patibulum* interchangeably to describe the gibbet used to suspend the bodies of the martyrs.
5 *Memoriale sanctorum* 2.2 (PL 115:770; CSM 2:402).
6 *Memoriale sanctorum* 2.1.1–2 (PL 115:766; CSM 2:398). *Indiculus luminosus* 3 (PL 121:518–9; CSM 1:275–6).
7 *Memoriale sanctorum* 2.1.2 (PL 115:766–7; CSM 2:398–9). Qur'ān 33.37.
8 *Memoriale sanctorum* 2.1 (PL 115:765–70; CSM 2:397–401); *Indiculus luminosus* 3 (PL 121:518–9; CSM 1:275–6).
9 *Memoriale sanctorum* 2.3 (PL 115:771; CSM 2:402).
10 Specifically for the pursuit of *liberales disciplinas*. Many of the martyrs came to Córdoba for the same reason, suggesting that the center of the emirate was also something of a center of Latin Christian culture.
11 *Memoriale sanctorum* 2.4 (PL 115:771–2; CSM 2:403–4).
12 *Memoriale sanctorum* 2.5–6 (PL 115:772–4; CSM 2:404–6).
13 Though the circumstances of their deaths are unknown, it would appear, given the fact that Artemia's husband had been a Muslim, that they were convicted of apostasy.
14 *Memoriale sanctorum* 2.8.9–10 (PL 115:838–40; CSM 2:412–13).
15 Unless Flora had more than one sister who shared her religious sentiments, she fled with Baldegotho, the recipient of one of Eulogius' extant letters. *Epistula* 2 (PL 115:844–5; CSM 2:497).
16 *Memoriale sanctorum* 2.8.13 (PL 115:841; CSM 2:414).
17 It is difficult to determine whether Maria was regarded as a blasphemer or an apostate. In her confession she said nothing about her mixed heritage as she reminded the judge that her brother had already been executed for blasphemy. Yet she, like Flora, was given the opportunity to become a Muslim and have the charges dropped. Most likely the judge, or Eulogius, wanted to simplify matters and treat them the same despite the difference in circumstances.
18 *Memoriale sanctorum* 2.9 (PL 115:776; CSM 2:415).
19 *Memoriale sanctorum* 2.10.1–4 (PL 115:777–8; CSM 2:416–17).
20 *Indiculus luminosus* 5 (PL 121:520; CSM 1:277–8); *Memoriale sanctorum* 1.9 (PL 115:746–7; CSM 2:377–8).
21 *Memoriale sanctorum* 2.10.10 (PL 115:781–2; CSM 2:419–20).
22 *Memoriale sanctorum* 2.10.11 (PL 115:782; CSM 2:421).
23 *Memoriale sanctorum* 2.10.23 (PL 115:786–7; CSM 2:425–6).
24 *Dhimmī* women were not, according to Islamic law, allowed to wear the veils worn by Muslim women. Lewis, p. 37. There is no way of knowing whether or not this proscription was in effect in Córdoba, but it would seem that the decision of Sabigotho and Liliosa not to cover their faces was, as much as their entering a church, a way of publicizing their rejection of Islam.
25 *Memoriale sanctorum* 2.10.34 (PL 115:791–2; CSM 2:430).

26 *Memoriale sanctorum* 2.11 (PL 115:792–3; CSM 2:430–1).
27 The two died on September 15. *Memoriale sanctorum* 2.12 (PL 115:793; CSM 2:431–2).
28 *Memoriale sanctorum* 2.13 (PL 115:793–5; CSM 2:432–3). As Eulogius reports, ʿAbd ar-Raḥmān II fell ill the moment he ordered the bodies of these two martyrs, who had been executed on September 16, to be burned. Ibid. 2.16.2 (PL 115:797; CSM 2:436).
29 *Memoriale sanctorum* 3.7 (PL 115:804–5; CSM 2:444–5).
30 *Memoriale sanctorum* 3.8–9 (PL 115:805–6; CSM 2:445–7).
31 Franz R. Franke, in his "Die freiwilligen Märtyrer von Cordova und das Verhältnis des Mozarabes zum Islam," *Spanische Forschungen des Görresgesellschaft* 13 (1953), p. 18, describes the monastery at Tabanos as a "Mittelpunkt" of the martyrs' movement.
32 *Memoriale sanctorum* 3.10 (PL 115:806–12; CSM 2:447–52).
33 *Memoriale sanctorum* 3.11 (PL 115:812–13; CSM 2:452–4).
34 *Memoriale sanctorum* 3.12 (PL 115:813–14; CSM 2:454).
35 *Memoriale sanctorum* 3.13 (PL 115:814; CSM 2:454–5). Peter was buried at Pinna Mellaria, and Louis, downriver from Córdoba at Palma. Amator's body was apparently never recovered.
36 *Memoriale sanctorum* 3.14 (PL 115:814; CSM 2:455).
37 *Memoriale sanctorum* 3.15 (PL 115:814–15; CSM 2:455).
38 The judge who struck Isaac was reprimanded by a *censor*. This may or may not have been the same position that Argimirus occupied.
39 *Memoriale sanctorum* 3.16 (PL 115:815; CSM 2:455–6).
40 *Memoriale sanctorum* 3.17 (PL 115:815–18; CSM 2:456–9)
41 *Liber apologeticus martyrum* 21–4 (PL 115:862–64; CSM 2: 488–90).
42 *Liber apologeticus martyrum* 25–35 (PL 115:864–70; CSM 2:490–6).
43 We will treat Eulogius' death in more detail in chapter 4.
44 Florez, 10:541. Justo Pérez de Urbel, in his *San Eulogio de Córdoba* (Madrid, 1928), p. 314, observes that the sisters may well have been Aurelius' daughters, whom he had placed in the care of the monastery at Tabanos prior to his confession. But then we would have expected Charles' envoy, who was looking specifically for information about Aurelʿus, to identify the two new martyrs as his daughters.
45 Samson, *Apologeticus* 2 pref., 9 (CSM 2:554).
46 Lévi-Provençal 1:231–2.
47 *Historia de los jueces*, p. 231.
48 Enrique Florez, et al., *España sagrada*, 52 vols. (Madrid, 1747–1918) 10:462–4. As Florez points out, the fact that the inscription identifies a martyr about whom nothing else is recorded, suggests that there may have been many martyrs about whom we know nothing at all.
49 Florez 23:230–5. Hroswitha (*c*.935–*c*.1000), a nun in the Saxon abbey of Gandersheim, composed, among her many works, a lyrical *Passio sancti Pelagii*. The fact that Otto I had commercial ties with the Cordoban caliphate lends credence to Hroswitha's claim that she relied on eyewitnesses, not on the account of Raguel, for her version. M. Gonsalva Wiegand, "The non-dramatic works of Hroswitha" (dissertation, St. Louis University, 1936), pp. 128–53.
50 Florez 10:564–70. In the *passio* Argentea's father is identified as Samuel. Arab sources allow for his identification as ʿUmar ibn Ḥafṣūn. Lévi-Provençal 2:21, note 1.

3   The martyrs of Córdoba and their historians

1   This chapter does not pretend to be an exhaustive survey of the secondary literature related to the martyrs. The emphasis here will be on the seminal works, treatments of the martyrs that feature a significant shift in interpretation from previous studies. Edward P. Colbert, "The martyrs of Córdoba (850–859): a study of the sources" (dissertation, Catholic University of America, 1962), pp. 1–16, refers to more works, but for the most part limits himself to a brief assessment of each author's sentiments regarding the propriety of the martyrs' actions.

2   Ambrosio de Morales, *Corónica general de España* . . ., ed. Benito Cano, 12 vols. (Madrid, 1791–2), 3:39.

3   For a complete biography of Ambrosio de Morales, see the appropriate section in: Rafael Ramírez de Arellano, *Ensayo de un catálogo biográfico de escritores de la provincia y diócesis de Córdoba*, 2 vols. (Madrid, 1922–3), 1:349–80.

4   Morales, 3:26. This was, of course, a very Renaissance thing to do. Curiously, both the ambassadors and Morales seem to have been unaware that, in the course of the previous century, other Spaniards had composed histories of their peoples: Sanchez de Aravalo (1470) in Latin, Diego de Valera (1482) in Castilian, and Tarafa (1543) in Catalan.

5   Morales, 7:256. As Morales admits, "this was one of the principal causes that motivated me to continue this chronicle forward from Pelayo," the Asturian warrior who handed the invading Muslims their first defeat and thus inaugurated the *reconquista.* Ibid., p. 257; see also pp. 274–5.

6   Morales, 7:264.

7   Juan de Mariana, *Historia general de España* (Madrid, 1789), p. 120.

8   Ibid., pp. 120–1. The eighteenth-century editor of the Valencia edition, interestingly enough, took issue with Mariana's interpretation because it seemed to place an inordinate amount of responsibility for the persecution on the Christians. Ibid., p. 121, n. 3.

9   Regarding Florez, see: Miguel Modino, "El P. Florez y la *España Sagrada*," *Hispania Sacra* 26 (1973): 7–20.

10   Florez, 10:336.

11   Simonet, p. 319.

12   Ibid., p. 379.

13   Louis Turquet de Mayerne, *Histoire générale d'Espagne*, trans. Edward Grimeston (London, 1612), p. 187. Some modernization of spelling and syntax.

14   Dozy 1:318.

15   Dozy 1:321.

16   Dozy 1:328.

17   Dozy 1:339.

18   Justo Pérez de Urbel, *San Eulogio de Córdoba* (Madrid, 1927), p. 19. Translated by a Benedictine of Stanbrook Abbey under the title, *A Saint Under Moslem Rule* (Milwaukee, 1937).

19   Modesto Lafuente y Zamalloa, *Historia general de España*, 2nd ed., 15 vols. (Madrid, 1869), 2:164.

20   Dozy 1:338.

21   Lévi-Provençal 1:226–7.

22 Pérez de Urbel, p. 243. See also: pp. 215, 246, 261.
23 Pérez de Urbel, p. 13.
24 Isidro de las Cagigas, *Los Mozárabes* (Madrid, 1947), pp. 194, 197.
25 Ricardo Garcia Villoslada, ed., *Historia de la Iglesia en España*, 5 vols. (Madrid, 1979–82), 2.1:49. Rafael Jiménez Pedrajas, "Las relaciones entre los cristianos y los musulmanes en Córdoba," *Boletín de la Real Academia de Córdoba de Ciencias, Bellas Letras y Nobles Artes* 80 (1960), p. 156. Emilio Linage Conde, "La mozarabía y Europa: en torno a San Eulogio y la regla de San Benito," *Historia mozárabe*, I Congreso Internacional de Estudios Mozárabes (Toledo, 1978), pp. 18–19.
26 Franke, p. 19.
27 Franke, p. 24.
28 Catholic University of America (Washington, D.C., 1962).
29 Colbert, pp. v, 6–7, 396–416.
30 *Muslim World* 55 (1965).
31 Cutler, pp. 329, 330.
32 Cutler, pp. 331.
33 Ibid.
34 Cutler, p. 322.
35 Pérez de Urbel, p. 14.
36 Jiménez Pedrajas, pp. 148, 156.
37 James Waltz, "The significance of the voluntary martyr movement of ninth-century Córdoba," *Muslim World* 60 (1970), p. 144, n. 6. Waltz had nothing positive to say about Cutler's treatment, prompting a rebuttal by Cutler at the 1983 Annual Meeting of the American Historical Association in San Francisco. Cutler's paper, "The revolutionary messianism of the ninth-century Spanish martyrs' movement," delivered before the Academy of Research Historians of Medieval Spain on December 28, reiterated his 1965 article, placing it within the context of previous and current Spanish historiography.
38 Waltz, p. 155.
39 Pérez de Urbel, pp. 193–4, also portrayed Eulogius as a man bothered and motivated by the decline of high Latin culture. As he saw it, however, it was specifically Eulogius' nationalism that led to his promotion of Latin learning and monasticism.
40 Waltz, p. 157.
41 Waltz, p. 226.
42 Waltz, pp. 228, 229.
43 Daniel, *Arabs and Medieval Europe*, p. 38.
44 For the fullest discussion of this problem of chronology, see Colbert, *Martyrs of Córdoba*, pp. 322–8.

4   The life of Eulogius

1 *Vita Eulogii* 1.2 (PL 115:707; CSM 1:331).
2 Eulogius' letter to bishop Wiliesindus mentions two sisters, Niola and Anulo, and three brothers, Alvarus, Isidorus, and Joseph. *Epistula* 3.1, 5, 8 (PL 115: 845, 847, 848; CSM 2:497, 499, 500).
3 *Liber apologeticus martyrum* 19 (PL 115:862; CSM 2:487).
4 *Vita Eulogii* 4.12 (PL 115:714; CSM 1:337). There is no reason why either Eulogius or Alvarus would have attempted to hide the former's mixed heritage

if such had indeed been the case. Alvarus admitted in a letter that his own ancestry was Jewish, and neither he nor Eulogius had anything but praise for the martyrs who were of mixed blood. Colbert, p. 349, mistakenly assumes that if Eulogius were related to Christophorus, both would have had to have Arab blood, and therefore treats the Christophorus that Alvarus mentioned as a completely different one than Eulogius' *contribulis*. Morales, in the notes to his edition of Eulogius' works (PL 115:726, n. 2), treated the two as one and the same without, however, drawing any conclusions about Eulogius' ancestry.

5 Toledo 4.24 (633) established the procedure by which young men were to be prepared for ecclesiastical service: ". . . If among the clerics there are any adolescent or pubescent boys, let them all dwell in one room of the atrium, so that they might pass through these treacherous years not in lust but in ecclesiastical discipline under an approved elder whom they shall have as both a master of doctrine and a living example." Vives, p. 201. We have already, in chapter 2, encountered many examples of Christians coming from all over southern Spain to study under the masters of the various *basilicae* in Córdoba. Some came of their own accord and some were dedicated by their parents. Apparently the latter had the option of returning to lay life when they reached the age of discretion. Alvarus, who, as we shall see below, was Eulogius' schoolmate, did not follow his friend into the priesthood. Similarly, both Emila and Hieremias studied together at the basilica of St. Cyprian, but only the former died an ecclesiastic.

6 Alvarus, *Epistula* 8 (CSM 1:203–10). The calendar of 961 lists Speraindeo under May 7, and uses the word "interfectio" to describe his death. Dozy, *Calendrier*. But it is extremely unlikely that he would have died a martyr without some indication in the writings of Eulogius and Alvarus. That he did not survive to see the martyrdoms of the 850s is evident from Alvarus' reference to his master as "bone recordationis memorie." *Vita Eulogii* 1.2 (PL 115:708; CSM 1:331).

7 *Memoriale sanctorum* 1.7 (PL 115:745; CSM 2:375–6). Deuteronomy 25.5, Matthew 27.29, and Luke 20.34–5.

8 *Vita Eulogii* 1.2 (PL 115:708; CSM 1:331).

9 "Zalla, Allah, Halla, Anabi. V. A. Zallen. Quod Latine dicitur, Psallat Deus super prophetam, et salvet eum." *Memoriale sanctorum* 2.1.3 (PL 115:767; CSM 2:399).

10 Isidore defined *juventus* as between the ages of 28 and 50. *Etymologies* 11.2. Toledo 4.20 (633) set the minimum age for deacons at 25, and for priests at thirty. Vives, p. 200.

11 *Vita Eulogii* 1.3 (PL 115:708; CSM 1:332). Eulogius described the martyrs Sanctius and Christophorus individually as "auditor noster," suggesting that they may have been students of his at one time.

12 *Vita Eulogii* 1.3 (PL 115:709; CSM 1:332).

13 *Epistula* 3 (PL 115:845; CSM 2:497).

14 *Annales Bertiniani*, ed. G. Waltz, MGH, Scriptores rerum germanicorum in usum scholarum . . . (Hanover, 1883), pp. 36, 38. *Fragmentum chronici Fontanellensis*, ed. George H. Pertz, MGH, Scriptores 2 (Hanover, 1829), pp. 302–3.

15 *Epistula* 3.1 (PL 115:845; CSM 2:498). Independent confirmation of this rebellion is not available.

16 Léonce Auzias, *L'Aquitaine carolingienne (778–987)*, Bibliothèque Méridionale,

series 2, vol. 28 (Toulouse, 1937), p. 264. Elie Lambert, "Le voyage de Saint Euloge dans les Pyrénées en 848," *Estudios dedicados a Menéndez Pidal*, vol. 4 (Madrid, 1953), pp. 557-67.

17 Colbert, p. 185.

18 *Annales Bertiniani*, pp. 36, 38. *Fragmentum chronici Fontanellensis*, pp. 302, 303.

19 Colbert's observation that Eulogius seems to have relied on second hand accounts of Perfectus' martyrdom and therefore must have been away from Córdoba at the time, would have been stronger had not Eulogius also credited others for his information about Pomposa. *Memoriale sanctorum* 3.11.3 (PL 115:812; CSM 2:453).

20 *Epistula* 3.10 (PL 115:849; CSM 2:501).

21 Ibid.

22 *Epistula* 3.9 (PL 115:848: CSM 2:500).

23 *Epistula* 3.12 (PL 115:850; CSM 2:502). Here, as elsewhere, it is difficult to determine whether or not Eulogius' use of the first person plural is rhetorical.

24 *Epistula* 3.13 (PL 115:852; CSM 2:503).

25 *Vita Eulogii* 2.4 (PL 115:709; CSM 1:332-3).

26 Ibid.

27 PL 115:733; CSM 2:364.

28 *Memoriale sanctorum* 2.1.5 (PL 115:769; CSM 2:401).

29 *Memoriale sanctorum* 1.9 (PL 115:747; CSM 2:377).

30 *Memoriale sanctorum* 1.17 (PL 115:751; CSM 2:381). Colbert, p. 218, regards this as a later insertion. But, as we shall see in the next chapter, there is no reason to suppose that Eulogius composed the apologetic portion of the work before recording the passions of the first group of eleven spontaneous martyrs.

31 *Vita Eulogii* 2.7 (PL 115:711; CSM 1:334).

32 *Vita Eulogii* 2.6 (PL 115:710; CSM 1:333-4).

33 *Vita Eulogii* 2.7 (PL 115:710-11; CSM 1:334).

34 We hear no more about Reccafredus after Eulogius' eucharistic threat. Given the way Alvarus referred to the "times of Reccafredus," he may well have died between the spring of 852 and the time Alvarus wrote the *Vita Eulogii*.

35 Though the date of Wistremirus' death has provoked considerable debate in the past, the fact that Eulogius, in his letter of November 851 to Bishop Wiliesindus of Pamplona, referred to Wistremirus as "adhuc vigentem" at the time of Eulogius' trip a year before, suggests that he died sometime in 851 prior to Eulogius' letter. Based on the chronology of the *Vita Eulogii*, the election most likely took place in early 852, not long after Eulogius' release from prison. *Epistula* 3.7 (PL 115:848; CSM 2:500). See Colbert, pp. 322-8, for a summary of the controversy.

36 *Vita Eulogii* 3.10 (PL 115:713; CSM 1:336). Possibly the political tensions that existed between Toledo and Córdoba at the time led to Eulogius' election *in absentia* as a form of protest. Dozy 1:354.

37 *Memoriale sanctorum* 2.14 (PL 115:795; CSM 2:433-4).

38 There has been little agreement among historians as to the precise date of this council. Eulogius tells us that the *exceptor* fell from the emir's grace *post bisseno mense* after the council met and *post aliquos menses* after the accession of Muḥammad I. Given that the council was intended to find a way of preventing future martyrdoms, it would make the most sense for it to have been convened immediately after a significant number of executions. The middle to late summer of 852, after the group of martyrs that died on July 27, fits best. It also makes the most sense in terms of the order of events that Eulogius described,

placing, as he did, the council on the eve of ʿAbd ar-Raḥmān II's death. The *exceptor*'s disgrace, then, would have occurred twelve months later, or roughly August, 853. It does not make as much sense to interpret *post bisseno mense* as "after the twelfth month," or December, as Colbert would have it (p. 249). *Memoriale sanctorum* 3.2 (PL 115:801; CSM 2:440).

39 *Memoriale sanctorum* 2.15.2 (PL 115:796; CSM 2:434–5).

40 *Vita Eulogii* 2.5 (PL 115:710; CSM 1:333), 3.8 (PL 115:711; CSM 1:335).

41 Eulogius tells us that he composed the *passio* of Aurelius, Sabigotho, et al., at the request of their youngest child nine months after the execution, that is, about May of 853. *Memoriale sanctorum* 2.10.17 (PL 115:784; CSM 2:423). We can assume that the others that followed in the summer of 852 were recorded at about the same time. At some point after Eulogius first terminated his martyrology with the account of Theodemirus' death and before the inclusion of the victims of the summer of 852, that is between November 851 and May 853, he incorporated the *passio* of Nunilo and Alodia, two Christians executed for apostasy in Bosca, the news of which he had received secondhand from Venerius, the bishop of Alcalá. He began the episode with an apology for his lack of prescience in ending his martyrology prematurely. *Memoriale sanctorum* 2.7 (PL 115:775; CSM 2:406). The *passio* of Flora and Maria was also composed sometime in this interim period. But its structure indicates that it was originally designed as a separate work, perhaps intended to accompany the *Documentum martyriale*, and was only later added to the rest of the *passiones*. *Memoriale sanctorum* 2.8 (PL 115:835–42; CSM 2:408–15).

42 *Memoriale sanctorum* 3, pref. (PL 115:799; CSM 2:438–9).

43 *Liber apologeticus martyrum* 22 (PL 115:863; CSM 2:488–9).

44 Aimoin, *De translatione* 1 (PL 115:941–8). Nathalia is, for some unknown reason, the name that Sabigotho assumed in the *passio* that accompanied the remains to Paris. The meeting between the monks and Eulogius is mentioned specifically in Aimoin 1.8 (PL 115:944–5).

45 Raphael Jiménez Pedrajas has made a case for regarding Eulogius as the author of the revised *passio* that Usuard and Odilard brought north with them, perhaps making this his last work. "San Eulogio de Córdoba, autor de la pasión francesa de los mártires mozárabes cordobeses Jorge, Aurelio y Natalia," *Anthologica Annua* 17 (1970).

46 *Vita Eulogii* 5.15 (PL 115:716; CSM 1:339).

47 *Vita Eulogii* 15 (PL 115:717; CSM 1:340).

5   Eulogius and the martyrs

1 *Vita Eulogii* 2.5 (PL 115:710; CSM 1:333).

2 *Epistula* 3.12 (PL 115:850; CSM 2:502).

3 *Memoriale sanctorum* 1.37 (PL 115:764; CSM 2:395).

4 *Memoriale sanctorum*, pref. letter (PL 115:732; CSM 2:364).

5 Hippolyte Delehaye, *Les Légendes hagiographiques*, 3rd ed. (Brussels, 1927), p. 11. Pierre Delooz, in his *Sociologie et canonisations*, Collection scientifique de la faculté de droit de l'Université de Liège, 30 (The Hague, 1969), p. 41, wrote: "The initiative always comes from below, that is to say, from a portion of the Christian people, and the authority never intervenes except to consecrate an initiative for which it was not originally responsible."

6 *Memoriale sanctorum* 2.8.9 (PL 115:839; CSM 2:412).

7 Dozy, *Le Calendrier*, September 27.

8 *Memoriale sanctorum*, pref. letter (PL 115:733; CSM 2:364).

9 Ibid.

10 Just as the Christians who lived in the cities, and hence in the closest proximity to Muslims, were most likely to recognize the social and economic advantages of conversion to Islam. Glick, p. 187. See also R. W. Bulliet's article, "Conversion to Islam and the Emergence of a Muslim Society in Iran," in Nehemiah Levtzion, ed., *Conversion to Islam* (New York, 1979), pp. 32–3.

11 So much so that the authorities became wary of the potential use of martyrial remains as relics. In the case of Rudericus and Salomon, they ordered the bodies tied to rocks before being cast into the river and even disposed of the stones that had been spattered with the victims' blood. *Liber apologeticus martyrum* 31 (PL 115:866; CSM 2:492).

12 Lawrence S. Cunningham, *The Meaning of Saints* (San Francisco, 1980), p. 44.

13 Delooz, p. 7, distinguishes between the "saint réel" and the "saint construit," the latter referring to the particular attributions of holiness on the part of the community (the "saint pour les autres"), which often obscure the identity of the historical, "réel" man. The exact relationship between the holy man and the community which ascribes holiness to him is far more difficult to conceptualize. Peter Brown, in "The rise and function of the holy man in late antiquity," *Journal of Roman Studies* 61 (1971), pp. 80–101, and more recently Raymond Van Dam, "Hagiography and history: the life of Gregory Thaumaturgus," *Classical Antiquity* 1 (1982), pp. 272–308, have described the holy man as a recognized intermediary between the community's everyday world and its "other world," whose appeal is based on the marginality of his existence and the duality of his sphere of activity. We can take this a step further. The success of the holy man depends on his ability to act in a manner diametrically opposed to the behavioral norms of his community and yet be applauded for it. The holy man's rejection of his society is interpreted as a positive attribute: the result of his virtuoso embodiment of the truths of the other world.

14 Daniel alludes to this in connection to Flora. *Arabs and Medieval Europe*, pp. 27–8, 38.

15 *Documentum martyriale* 21 (PL 115:871; CSM 2:472). See also: *Memoriale sanctorum* 2.8.8 (PL 115:821; CSM 2:411–12).

16 *Vita Eulogii* 2.4 (PL 115:709. CSM 1:332–3). See also: *Documentum martyriale*, prol. (PL 115:821; CSM 2:461).

17 Donald Riddle, *The Martyrs, a Study in Social Control* (Chicago, 1931). See especially chapter 1.

18 Eulogius seems to have been quite familiar with this genre, perhaps specifically with its North American renditions, such as Tertullian's *Ad martyras*, and Cyprian's *De gloria martyrii*.

19 *Documentum martyriale* 23 (PL 115:832; CSM 2:473); 14 (PL 115:828; CSM 2:468–9).

20 *Documentum martyriale* 23 (PL 115:832: CSM 2:473).

21 *Documentum martyriale* 21 (PL 115:831; CSM 2:472).

22 *Documentum martyriale* 1 (PL 115:822; CSM 2:462).

23 *Documentum martyriale* 18 (PL 115:830; CSM 2:471). Genesis 19:30.

24 *Documentum martyriale* 14 (PL 115:827–8; CSM 2:468).

25 *Documentum martyriale* 25 (PL 115:833; CSM 2:474).

26 *Epistula* 1.3 (PL 115:844; CSM 2:496). See also: *Memoriale sanctorum* 2.8.16 (PL 115:842; CSM 2:415); *Vita Eulogii* 2.4 (PL 115:709; CSM 1:333).

27 *Memoriale sanctorum* 2.10.10 (PL 115:781; CSM 2:419–20).

28 *Memoriale sanctorum* 2.10.18 (PL 115:785; CSM 2:423).
29 *Memoriale sanctorum* 2.10.28 (PL 115:789; CSM 2:428).
30 *Memoriale sanctorum* 2.11.2 (PL 115:792; CSM 2:431).
31 *Memoriale sanctorum* 2.10.24 (PL 115:787; CSM 2:426).
32 Eulogius described Sanctius and Christophorus each as *auditor noster*, which
   would seem to indicate that they were at one time students of the *magister*.
   Christophorus was also a *contribulis* of the priest, as were Paulus and Ludovicus.
   Memoriale sanctorum 2.3 (PL 115:771; CSM 2:402), 2.6 (PL 115:773; CSM
   2:405), 2.11 (PL 115:792; CSM 2:430), 3.13 (PL 115:814; CSM 2:455).
33 *Vita Eulogii* 2.3 (PL 115:708; CSM 1:332).
34 *Vita Eulogii* 2.3 (PL 115:710–11; CSM 1:332). It is true, as Alvarus records,
   that Eulogius composed rules for the monks (*regulas fratrum componere*). The
   priest himself reports that he provided Leocritia with one. But this was a service
   that early medieval ecclesiastics regularly performed in the days before
   monasticism had achieved the institutional uniformity that would character-
   ize it in later centuries, and does not imply any special involvement on
   Eulogius' part. See chapter 9 below for a fuller discussion of ninth-century
   monasticism in Córdoba.
35 *Epistula* 3.10 (PL 115:849; CSM 2:501). *Memoriale sanctorum* 1.1 (PL 115:739;
   CSM 2:369).
36 *Memoriale sanctorum* 1.38 (PL 115:765; CSM 2:396). *Epistula* 3.10 (PL 115:849;
   CSM 2:501). See also: *Documentum martyriale* 11 (PL 115:849; CSM 2:467).
37 *Memoriale sanctorum* 1.4 (PL 115:741; CSM 2:371).
38 *Memoriale sanctorum* 1.3–4 (PL 115:740–1; CSM 2:371–2).

6   Martyrdom without miracles

1 Angel Fábrega Grau, *Pasionario hispánico*, 2 vols., Monumenta Hispaniae
  Sacra, serie litúrgica, 6 (Barcelona, 1953). Early medieval Christians,
  especially the heirs of the Visigoths, set great store by the liturgy as an
  authoritative basis for doctrinal argument: *lex orandi, lex credendi*. M. C. Díaz y
  Díaz, in his article "Literary aspects of the Visigothic liturgy," in Edward
  James, ed., *Visigothic Spain: New Approaches* (Oxford, 1980), p. 72, described the
  non-biblical texts within the Visigothic liturgy as "... condensed formulations
  of doctrines, moral norms, and hagiographical accounts," intended more for
  the rumination of the educated cleric than the edification of the congregation.
  As such they were considered sufficiently precise and authoritative for use in
  doctrinal debates. From the perspective of each of the participants in the
  debate, then, the fact that the Cordoban martyrs did not exactly fit the
  patterns established by the passionary was a serious problem.
2 Fábrega Frau, *Pasionario* 2:12–13.
3 Ibid.
4 The only criticism leveled against the martyrs that was not based on the
  passionary paradigm was the observation that the martyrs' bodies, which were
  typically left exposed after decapitaion, were not immune to the processes of
  decomposition. *Memoriale sanctorum* 1.26 (PL 115:758; CSM 2:389).
5 *Memoriale sanctorum* 1.12 (PL 115:748; CSM 2:379). See also: *Liber apologeticus
  martyrum* 7 (PL 115:856; CSM 2:479–80).
6 Henry Davis, in his edition of the *Liber regulae pastoralis*, Ancient Christian
  Writers 11 (Westminster, Maryland, 1950), p. 8, rightly emphasizes the often
  overlooked *regula* aspect of the work. Gregory's intention was to provide
  bishops with their own "rule" to govern their lives in the world.
7 *Liber regulae pastoralis* 1.5, p. 31.

8 Gregory, *Dialogues*, trans. Odo J. Zimmerman, Fathers of the Church 39 (Washington, D.C., 1959), p. 5.

9 Gregory, *Dialogues*, p. 51.

10 Gregory, *Dialogues*, p. 52. Compare Sulpicius Severus, *Letter to Eusebius.* Matthew 14.29; Acts 27.14.

11 Gregory, *Dialogues*, pp. 13, 19–20, 27, 146–7.

12 The monk of Whitby, who composed the earliest known life of Gregory, followed his subject's example when he claimed that miracles were unnecessary for an attribution of sanctity, only to list numerous examples of such phenomena associated with Gregory. For the translated text, see: Charles W. Jones, *Saints' Lives and Chronicles in Early Medieval England* (Ithaca, New York, 1947).

13 Gregory, *Dialogues*, p. 52.

14 *Memoriale sanctorum* 1.15 (PL 115:750; CSM 2:380–1). Luke 10.20.

15 *Liber apologeticus martyrum* 9, 10 (PL 115:857; CSM 2:481). Eulogius took the same basic tack when addressing the criticism that the martyrs' bodies were not immune to decay: "The adversaries object to the corruption of the martyrs' bodies. But, I pray, let them answer what difference this makes to those bestowed with the heavenly reward; as if the martyrs – who were well aware of the sentence suffered by mortals, as stated to Adam, 'You are dust and into dust shall you return,' and who knew that they would be handed over to be killed by the tyrant's punishments in order to achieve the desired end – were aspiring to some honor of the flesh" *Memoriale sanctorum* 1.26 (PL 115:758; CSM 2:389); Genesis 3.19. After giving examples of biblical characters like Job and Lazarus who were clearly susceptible to the ravages of disease, he bade his opponents ". . . review the shining deeds of the victories of the rest of the holy men, as numerous as the stars in the sky, and then let the impious insult, if they dare, their putrid members, consumed with the pains and punishments of their torment. This temporal corruption of bodies in no way infers detriment to the soul of the holy . . ." *Memoriale sanctorum* 1.26 (PL 115:758–9; CSM 2:389–90); Isaiah 40.6; Acts 2.29; 2.7–8; and Luke 16.20. Eulogius seems to have taken some license with Acts 2.31, which in the Vulgate ends, ". . . neque caro eius vidit corruptionem," not ". . . et caro eius vidit corruptionem," and which refers not to David but to Christ.

16 Eulogius did know the *Moralia in Iob*. *Memoriale sanctorum* 1.13 (PL 115:748; CSM 2:379).

17 *Memoriale sanctorum* 2.1.5 (PL 115:769; CSM 2:400–1). Eulogius also regarded the death of ʿAbd ar-Raḥmān II as an act of divine vengeance. Ibid., 2.16.2 (PL 115:797; CSM 2:436).

18 *Memoriale sanctorum* 2.12 (PL 115:793; CSM 2:432).

19 *Liber apologeticus martyrum* 31 (PL 115:866; CSM 2:402).

20 *Memoriale sanctorum* pref., 4–5 (PL 115:738; CSM 2:368–9).

21 *Memoriale sanctorum* 2.10.12 (PL 115:782; CSM 2:421); 2.10.20 (PL 115:785; CSM 2:424); 3.8.2 (PL 115:805; CSM 2:446); 2.5 (PL 115:773; CSM 2:404).

22 Peter L. Berger, *The Sacred Canopy* (New York, 1969), pp. 43–5, uses the term "plausibility structure" to indicate the propensity of a given audience to accept a particular way of looking at their world. Applying this same principle in a more individualized way to the witnesses of a miracle, Delahaye, *Légendes*, p. 11, noted that a witness, asked to describe what he had just seen, could offer nothing more objective than his own "legend," based on fact but embellished according to his particular impressions, feelings, sympathies, etc.

23 Peter Brown observed, in reference to relics, that "the supernatural becomes the depository of the objectified values of the group." "Society and the supernatural: a medieval change," *Daedalus* 104 (1975), p. 141.

24 Gregory of Tours illustrated this process when he wrote: "Some ask whether we should say the *life* of the saints or the *lives* of the saints . . . It is clear that it is better to talk about the life of the Fathers than the lives, because though there may be some difference in their merits, and virtues, yet the life of one body nourished them all in the world." *Liber vitae patrum*, quoted by Jones, *Saints' Lives*, p. 62.

25 It is possible, but exceedingly difficult to verify, that the more assimilated Christians were unreceptive to miracle activity as a result of the influence of Islamic doctrine, which did not officially recognize such miracles.

26 There are exceptions. Since Perfectus' martyrdom preceded the spontaneous martyrdoms by more than a year, we would expect there to be enough sympathy in the Christian community to recognize miracles. The initial support that the earliest spontaneous martyrs enjoyed prior to the clerical arrests accounts for the signs and portents that graced Isaac's birth and childhood. *Memoriale sanctorum* pref., 4–5 (PL 115:738; CSM 2:368–9).

27 *Memoriale sanctorum* 1.14 (PL 115:749; CSM 2:380).

28 *Liber apologeticus martyrum* 7 (PL 115:850; CSM 2:480).

29 Origen, *Contra Celsum* 2.49, trans. Henry Chadwick (Cambridge, 1953), p. 103.

30 Augustine, *City of God* 22.8.

31 *Memoriale sanctorum* 1.13 (PL 115:748–9; 379–80).

32 *Memoriale sanctorum* 1.14 (PL 115:749–50; CSM 2:380).

7   *Martyrdom without pagans*

1 *Liber apologeticus martyrum* 12 (PL 115:857; CSM 2:481).

2 Most previous historians have completely missed the point of this objection. Pérez de Urbel, for example, wrote: "The Christians, for their part, did not pay much attention to the Muslim teachings. Living amongst the Arabs and rubbing elbows with them on a daily basis, they disregarded their religion and despised their culture." *San Eulogio*, p. 67. Franke, p. 15, more accurately observed that al-Andalus was characterized by a "pervasive religious indifference."

3 *Liber apologeticus martyrum* 17–18 (PL 115:860–1; CSM 1:486).

4 Ibid. Galatians 1.9.

5 Ibid.

6 *Liber apologeticus martyrum* 19 (PL 115:861; CSM 2:487).

7 Eulogius thus becomes the first identifiable Latin ecclesiastic to assess Islam as a religious phenomenon. See my article, "The earliest Spanish Christian views of Islam," *Church History* 55 (1986), pp. 281–93. For a recent treatment of early Greek Christian views of Islam, see: John Moorhead, "The earliest Christian theological response to Islam," *Religion* 11 (1981), 265–74.

8 The exile of Hilary to Phrygia in 356 exposed him to all of the theological intricacies of the Arian conflict. His writings provided subsequent generations of Latin ecclesiastics with a vocabulary for dealing with later Christological heresies.

9 *Liber apologeticus martyrum* 19 (PL 115:861; CSM 2:487).

10 Matthew 7.15, 24.11, 24.24, etc. Eulogius was not the first Christian author to describe Islam as a heresy, or Muḥammad as a false prophet. John of

Damascus, whose depiction of the "Ishmaelites" in his treatise on heresies proved paradigmatic for generations of Greek Christians trying to cope with Islam, preceded him by more than a century. See: D. J. Sahas, *John of Damascus on Islam: The "Heresy of the Ishmaelites"* (Leiden, 1972); A. Khoury, *Polémique byzantine contre l'Islam: VIIe au XIIIe siècles* (Leiden, 1972).

11 *Memoriale sanctorum* 1.7 (PL 115:744; CSM 2:375), 2.1.2 (PL 115:766–7; CSM 2:398–9).

12 *Memoriale sanctorum* 1.7 (PL 115:744–5; CSM 1:375–6).

13 *Memoriale sanctorum* 2.1.2 (PL 115:766–7; CSM 2:398–9). Qur'ān S.33.37.

14 *Memoriale sanctorum* 1.7 (PL 115:745; CSM 2:376). Cf. *Memoriale sanctorum* 2.1.2 (PL 115:766–7; CSM 2:398).

15 *Liber apologeticus martyrum* 16 (PL 115:859–60; CSM 2:483–6).

16 Daniel 7:23–5.

17 *Indiculus luminosus* 21 (PL 121:535; CSM 1:293–4). Alvarus was the first Latin author to transform Muḥammad into antichrist. Beatus of Liébana, the eighth-century Spanish author of the most popular commentary on Revelation, never mentioned Islam or its prophet.

18 *Indiculus luminosus* 21 (PL 121:536; CSM 1:294–5). Alvarus placed the beginning of Muḥammad's reign in 625. Eulogius, on the basis of the Leyre biography, had the prophet "rise up" in 618.

19 Daniel 11.36, 38. *Indiculus luminosus* 25 (PL 121:540; CSM 1:298). Alvarus may have been playing on the similarities between Maozim and muezzin (*muadhdhin*), but it would be a mistake to suppose that he was ignorant of the difference. Daniel, *Arabs and Medieval Europe*, pp. 41–2.

20 *Indiculus luminosus* 23 (PL 121:538; CSM 1:296–7).

21 *Indiculus luninosus* 24 (PL 121:539; CSM 1:297–8).

22 *Indiculus luminosus* 26 (PL 121:542; CSM 1:301), 30 (PL 121:548; CSM 1:307).

23 Richard W. Southern, *Western Views of Islam in the Middle Ages* (Cambridge, Mass., 1962), p. 22.

24 *Indiculus luminosus* 34–35 (PL 121:553; CSM 1:312–13). I John 2.18: "Even now there are many antichrists."

25 From late antiquity, "antichrist" had two quite distinct meanings. The book of Revelation was the main source for the concept of a specific antichrist that would play a key role in ushering in the Last Days. But from the time of Tertullian (see, for example, *Adversus Marcionem* 5.16), Christian leaders also adopted a more general usage of the term based on 1 John 2.22 – "He is the Antichrist who denies the Father and the Son" (cf. 1 John 2.18, 4.2–3; 2 John 1.7) – and applied it to heretics. It proved an especially popular epithet for those ecclesiastics, like Arius and Nestor, whose Christological views contradicted the formulae of the ecumenical councils. Hilary wrote of Arius: "When you preach the Father and Son as Creator and Creature, do you think that you can avoid, through disguised names, being regarded as antichrist?" *De trinitate*, 6.42 (PL 10:191). Isidore of Seville included both the specific and general meanings of the term in *Etymologies* 8.11.20–2). For more information about antichrist, see: Richard Kenneth Emmerson, *Antichrist in the Middle Ages: A Study of Medieval Apocalypticism, Art and Literature* (Seattle, 1981).

26 Dozy 1:319.

27 Southern, pp. 25–6.

28 Glick, p. 176.

8 *Martyrdom without persecution*

1 *Liber apologeticus martyrum* 3 (PL 115:853–4; CSM 2:477).
2 *Memoriale sanctorum* 1 pref., 3 (PL 115:737; CSM 2:367). Eulogius also seemed surprised when reporting that Hieremia was whipped and Leovigildus struck. *Memoriale sanctorum* 2.4 (PL 115:772; CSM 2:404), 2.11 (PL 115:793; CSM 2:431).
3 *Liber apologeticus martyrum* 5–6 (PL 115:854–5; CSM 2:478–9). Psalm 115:15.
4 *Memoriale sanctorum* 1.18 (PL 115:751; CSM 2:382).
5 Ignatius of Antioch, *Letter to the Romans* 4–5, Alexander Roberts and James Donaldson, eds., *Ante-Nicene Fathers*, 10 vols. (New York, 1903), 1:75–6.
6 Evarestus, *Life of Polycarp* 1, *Ante-Nicene Fathers* 1:39.
7 W. H. C. Frend, *Martyrdom and Persecution in the Early Church: A Study of the Conflict from the Macabees to Donatus* (Oxford, 1965), ch. 12.
8 Peter Hinchliff, *Cyprian of Carthage and the Unity of the Christian Church* (London, 1974).
9 W. H. C. Frend, *The Donatist Church* (Oxford, 1952).
10 *Memoriale sanctorum* 1.23 (PL 115:757; CSM 2:388). Acts 21:10–14.
11 *Memoriale sanctorum* 24 (PL 115:758; CSM 2:389).
12 Fábrega Grau, *Pasionario*, 2:266–79, 233–7, 328–31. Eulogius also mentioned Babylas of Antioch (pp. 196–202), Thyrsus of Nicomedia (pp. 202–20), and Sabastian (pp. 148–76).
13 Fábrega Grau, *Pasionario* 2:133.
14 Fábrega Grau, *Pasionario* 2:47.
15 *Memoriale sanctorum* 1.21 (PL 115:754–5; CSM 2:385–6). Cf., *Indiculus luminosus* 6–7 (PL 121:520–2; CSM 1:278–9). According to Lewis, p. 34, such concern about pollution was rare in the Islamic West.
16 *Documentum martyriale* 18 (PL 115:829–30; CSM 2:470).
17 This strategy is even more obvious in Alvarus' apologetics. The first section of the *Indiculus luminosus* is, in part, a portrait of Andalusian persecution in which Perfectus and Joannes are the key figures. Only after painting this backdrop did Alvarus refer to the heroic resistance of Isaac. *Indiculus luminosus* 12 (PL 121:527; CSM 1:285).
18 *Memoriale sanctorum* 2.1.6 (PL 115:769–70; CSM 2:401). Cf., *Memoriale sanctorum* 1.10 (PL 115:747; CSM 2:378).
19 *Epistula* 3.10 (PL 115:849; CSM 2:501).
20 *Memoriale sanctorum* 3.3 (PL 115:801–2; CSM 2:441).
21 *Memoriale sanctorum* 1.20 (PL 115:753; CSM 2:384).

9 *The martyrs and their motives*

1 *Memoriale sanctorum* pref., 2, 6 (PL 115:736, 738; CSM 2:367, 369).
2 *Memoriale sanctorum* 2.2 (PL 115:770; CSM 2:402).
3 *Memoriale sanctorum* 3.10.2 (PL 115:807; CSM 2:447). In Toledo 6.6 (638), "propositum" refers to the vow taken by those who voluntarily assume the *habitum religiosum* and/or associate themselves with some religious institution. Vives, p. 238.
4 Toledo 1.2 (397–400), Vives, p. 20: "When we speak of penitents we mean those who after baptism have been reconciled before the divine altar, having done public penance dressed in a robe, on account of murder or other serious

crimes and sins." For a general treatment of the subject, see: Severino Gonzáles Rivas, S.J., *La penitencia en la primitiva iglesia española* (Salamanca, 1949).

5 Toledo 3.11 (589), Vives, p. 128: ". . . let him who had repented of his sin first be suspended from communion and, with the other penitents, be made to receive the imposition of the hands."

6 Thomas N. Tentler, *Sin and Confession on the Eve of the Reformation* (Princeton, 1977), p. 4.

7 Council of Elvira 7 (300–6), Vives, p. 3: "If any of the faithful, after having committed fornication and having done the necessary penance, should fornicate again, he shall not have communion even at the end of his life." As Tentler, p. 5, points out, expulsion from the Christian community was a logical way of dealing with discipline problems while the church was still an exclusive community. The need for a system of reconciliation followed closely upon the conversion of the empire, when the church was adjusting to its new role as an inclusive religious body.

8 Council of Barcelona 1.6–7 (540), Vives, p. 53: "Male penitents who wear the tonsure and religious habit shall pass the rest of their lives in prayer and fasting. Penitents shall not attend parties, nor give themselves over to business, whether it be in giving or receiving, but rather dedicate themselves to a frugal life in their own homes."

9 R. C. Mortimer, *The Origins of Private Penance in the Western Church* (Oxford, 1939), p. 2.

10 Gerard Gilles Meersseman, "I penitenti nei secoli XI e XII," *I laici nelle "societas christiana" dei secoli XI e XII*. Pubblicazione dell'Università Cattolica del Sacro Cuore. Miscellanea del Centro di Studi Medievali, vol. 5. (Milan, 1965), p. 309. Though Meersseman focuses on the eleventh and twelfth centuries, his article begins with an overview of the late antique origins of medieval penitential practices.

11 Isidore, *Sententiae* 2.13, 15; *De Eccl. officiis* 2.9, 17. Carleton M. Sage, "Paul Albar of Córdoba: Studies of his life and writings" (dissertation, Catholic University of America, 1943), p. 106, n. 10. Barcelona 1.8 (540), specifically requiring those who recovered from their illness after receiving penance to remain penitents, attests to the frequency of the practice (Vives, p. 53). Gonzáles Rivas, *La penitencia*, pp. 113–18.

12 Augustine, *De poenitentibus* (PL 39:1713–15); "Do you wish to free yourself from doubt? Do penance while you are healthy." Quoted by Tentler, p. 9.

13 Toledo 4.54 (633), Vives, p. 209. The earliest precise conciliar reference in Spain: the second council of Barcelona (599), Vives, p. 160.

14 Toledo 4.55 (633), Vives, p. 632.

15 Toledo 4.55, 56 (633), Vives, p. 210; Toledo 6.6 (638), Vives, p. 238; Toledo 10.5, 6 (656), Vives, p. 312–13.

16 Toledo 6.6 (638) Vives, p. 238: ". . . any men or women who at one time or another spontaneously donned the *habitum religiosum*, or any man dedicated to the choir of a church, or any woman dedicated to a monastery of women who prevaricates shall be obliged against his or her will to return to the former *propositum* . . ."

17 Leander, *Regula ad Florentiana sororem suam* 17 (PL 72:890).

18 There is a marked and misleading tendency among historians of early medieval monasticism to treat these institutions as more formal and uniform than they actually were. In their search for the first traces of Benedictine influence in the Iberian peninsula, Spanish scholars have largely ignored the

indigenous traditions and interesting local variations. As Antonio Linage Conde observed in his *El Monacato en España e Hispanoamérica* (Salamanca, 1977), p. 23, efforts to understand early medieval monasticism have been hampered by a "proyección anacronística" of modern notions of the religious life to a remote past. José Orlandis, *Estudios sobre instituciones monásticas medievales* (Pamplona, 1971), is an exception to this rule. Working closely with the sources, Orlandis presents a whole spectrum of monastic alternatives each reflecting the particular spiritual needs and physical means of its founder.

19 E. John, "'Secularium Prioratus' and the Rule of St. Benedict," *Revue bénédictine* 75 (1965), pp. 212–39.

20 In the case of Tabanos, the families of both Elisabeth and Hieremia were involved in its foundation. Yet given the fact that Elisabeth served as abbess and her brother Martinus as abbot, it is likely that the land upon which the monastery rested was a part of her family's holdings.

21 Typical are Seville 2.10 (619), Vives, pp. 169–70, and Toledo 4.51 (633), Vives, pp. 208–9. As Orlandis has noted, p. 133, the examples of canons aimed at curbing abuses by the lay founders of monasteries and churches are, in comparison, few and far between. Council of Lérida (540), Vives, p. 56.

22 Fructuosus, *Regula monastica communis* 1 (PL 87:1111).

23 Ibid.

24 *Memoriale sanctorum* 2.2 (PL 115:770; CSM 2:402).

25 *Memoriale sanctorum* 3.10.2 (PL 115:807; CSM 2:447).

26 *Memoriale sanctorum* 3.10.4–5 (PL 115:808; CSM 2:448).

27 *Memoriale sanctorum* 3.10.10 (PL 115:810; CSM 2:450–1). Matthew 11:12.

28 *Memoriale sanctorum* 2.10.7 (PL 115:779; CSM 2:418).

29 Ibid. Franke, p. 24, regards ths case of Aurelius and Sabigotho as the best example of the connection between asceticism and martyrdom. He did not, however, recognize the institutionalized penitential basis of the couple's regimen.

30 *Memoriale sanctorum* 2.10.9 (PL 115:780; CSM 2:419).

31 *Memoriale sanctorum* 2.10.12–13 (PL 115:782–3; CSM 2:421–2).

32 *Memoriale sanctorum* 3.7.3 (PL 115:804; CSM 2:444).

33 *Memoriale sanctorum* 2.8.3 (PL 115:836; CSM 2:409).

34 *Memoriale sanctorum* 2.8.9 (PL 115:839; CSM 2:412). In other cases, it is more difficult to make the connection between martyrdom and penitential anxiety. Seven of the priests who died as spontaneous martyrs had no known monastic connections and were, as a result of their clerical status, not permitted access to the normal public penitential process. But these very restrictions, combined with the fact that secular clerical duty was universally considered less conducive to personal sanctification than monastic withdrawal from the world, may in themselves have led spiritually sensitive priests to their deaths once Isaac had provided them with such an effective way of overcoming the limitations of their office.

35 *Memoriale sanctorum* 1.6 (PL 115:743; CSM 2:374).

36 *Memoriale sanctorum* 1.15 (PL 115:750; CSM 2:381).

37 *Memoriale sanctorum* 2.15.1 (PL 115:795; CSM 2:434).

38 *Historia de los jueces*, p. 232.

39 The importance of precedent as the "generator" of the martyrs' movement is apparent in the frequency with which individual martyrs were influenced by the example of a friend or relative who had already been martyred. Dozy, 1:328.

40 Tritton's chapter on non-Muslims in government service is full of references not only to the ubiquity of the practice but the regularity of purges in response to criticism by Muslims who regarded such practices as abhorrent. See especially ʿUmar II's letter to this effect, pp. 21–2.

41 Daniel (*Arabs and Medieval Europe*, pp. 25–6), too, sees Isaac's decision to retire – a decision stemming from "emotional and perhaps mental imbalance," caused by conflicts between his Christian identity and his vocation – as a key component in his decision to seek martyrdom.

Select Bibliography

Aigrain, René. *L'Hagiographie: ses sources, ses méthodes, son histoire.* Paris: 1953.

Aimoin, *De translatione SS. martyrum Georgii monachi, Aurelii et Nathaliae, ex urbe Corduba Parisios.* PL 115:941–8.

Alvarus, Paulus. *Epistula.* PL 121:411–514; CSM 1:144–270.

Indiculus luminosus. PL 115:513–56; CSM 1:270–315.

Vita Eulogii. PL 115:705–20; CSM 1:330–43.

Arjona Castro, Antonio. *Anales de Córdoba Musulmana.* Córdoba: 1983.

El reino de Córdoba durante la dominación musulmana. Córdoba: 1982.

Ashtor, Eliyahu. *The Jews of Moslem Spain.* Philadelphia: 1973.

Berger, Peter. *The Sacred Canopy.* New York: 1969.

Brown, Peter. *The Cult of the Saints.* Chicago: 1981.

"The rise and function of the holy man in late antiquity." *Journal of Roman Studies* 61 (1971), pp. 80–101.

"Society and the supernatural: a medieval change." *Daedalus* 104 (1975).

CSM: *Corpus scriptorum muzarabicorum.* Edited by Juan Gil. 2 vols. Madrid: 1973.

Cagigas, Isidro de las. *Los mozárabes.* Madrid: 1947.

Cantarino, Vicente. *Entre monjes y musulmanes: el conflicto que fue España.* Madrid: 1978.

Chejne, Anwar G. *Muslim Spain: Its History and Culture.* Minneapolis: 1974.

Chronica muzarabica. CSM 1:15–54.

Colbert, Edward P. "The Martyrs of Córdoba (850–859): A Study of the Sources." Dissertation, Catholic University of America, 1962.

Collins, Roger. *Early Medieval Spain: Unity and Diversity, 400–1000.* New York: 1983.

Cunningham, Lawrence S. *The Meaning of Saints.* San Francisco: 1980.

Cutler, Allan. "The Ninth-century Spanish martyrs' movement and the origins of Western Christian missions to the Muslims." *Muslim World* 55 (1965), pp. 321–39.

Daniel, Norman. *The Arabs and Medieval Europe.* 2nd ed. New York: 1979.

Islam and the West: The Making of an Image. Edinburgh: 1960.

Delahaye, Hippolyte. *Les Légendes hagiographiques.* 3rd ed. Brussels: 1927.

Delooz, Pierre. *Sociologie et canonisations.* Collection scientifique de la faculté de droit de l'Université de Liège, 30. The Hague: 1969.

Dennet, D. C. *Conversion and the Poll Tax in Early Islam.* Harvard Historical Monographs, 22. Cambridge, Massachusetts: 1950.

Díaz y Díaz, M. C. "Literary aspects of the Visigothic liturgy." *Visigothic Spain: New Approaches.* Edited by Edward James. Oxford: 1980.

Dozy, Reinhart P. A. *Le Calendrier de Cordoue.* Translated by C. Pellat. 2nd ed. Medieval Iberian Peninsula Texts and Studies, 1. Leyden: 1961.

Histoire des musulmans d'Espagne jusqu'à la conquête de l'Andalousie par les almoravides. 3 vols. Revised by Evariste Lévi-Provençal. Leiden: 1932.

Dubois, Jacques. *Le martyrologie d'Usuard: texte et commentaire.* Subsidia hagiographica, 40. Brussels: 1965.

Emmerson, Richard K. *Antichrist in the Middle Ages: A Study of Medieval Apocalypticism, Art and Literature.* Seattle: 1981.

Eulogius. *Documentum martyriale.* PL 115:819–34; CSM 2:459–75.

Epistula. PL 115:841–52; CSM 2:495–503.

Liber apologeticus martyrum. PL 115:851–70; CSM 2:475–95.

Memoriale sanctorum. PL 115:751–818; CSM 2:363–459.

Fábrega Grau, Angel. *Pasionario hispánico.* 2 vols. Monumenta Hispaniae Sacra, serie litúrgica, 6. Barcelona: 1953.

Fattel, Antoine. *Le statut légal des non-musulmans en pays d'Islam.* Beirut: 1958.

Florez, Enrique, et al. *España Sagrada.* 52 vols. Madrid: 1747–1918.

Franke, Franz R. "Die freiwilligen Märtyrer von Cordova und das Verhältnis des Mozarabes zum Islam (nach den Schriften von Speraindeo, Eulogius und Alvar)." *Spanische Forschungen des Görresgesellschaft,* 13 (1953), pp. 1–170.

Frend, W. H. C. *The Donatist Church.* Oxford: 1952.

Martyrdom and Persecution in the Early Church: A Study of the Conflict from the Macabees to Donatus. Oxford: 1965.

Gaiffier, Baudouin. "Les notices hispaniques du martyrologe romain." *Analecta Bollandiana* 58 (1940), pp. 79–89.

Garcia Villoslada, Ricardo, ed. *Historia de la Iglesia en España.* 5 vols. Madrid: 1979–82.

Gil, Juan. "Judíos y cristianos en la hispania del siglo VII." *Hispania Sacra* 30 (1977), pp. 9–110.

"Judios y cristianos en hispania (s. VIII y IX)." *Hispania Sacra* 31 (1978–9), pp. 9–88.

Glick, Thomas. *Islamic and Christian Spain in the Early Middle Ages.* Princeton: 1979.

Gonzáles Rivas, Severino, S. J. *La penitencia en la primitiva iglesia española.* Salamanca: 1949.

Gregory. *Dialogues.* Translated Odo J. Zimmerman. Fathers of the Church, 39. Washington, D.C.: 1959.

Liber regulae pastoralis. Translated by Henry Davis. Ancient Christian Writers, 11. Westminster, Maryland: 1950.

Guichard, Pierre. *Al-Andalus: estructura antropológica de una sociedad islámica en occidente.* Barcelona: 1970.

Halpern, Charles J. "The ideology of silence: Prejudice and pragmatism on the medieval religious frontier." *Comparative Studies in Society and History* 26 (1984), pp. 442–66.

Hinchliff, Peter. *Cyprian of Carthage and the Unity of the Christian Church.* London: 1974.

Historia de la conquista de España por Abenalcotía. Translated by Julián Ribera. Madrid: 1926.

Historia de los jueces de Córdoba por Aljoxani. Translated by Julián Ribera. Madrid: 1926.

Historia mozárabe. Ponencias y comunicaciones presentadas al I Congreso Internacional de Estudios Mozárabes. Toledo: 1979.

Hodgson, Marshall G. S. *The Venture of Islam.* 3 vols. New York: 1972.

The Holy Qur'an. Translated by A. Yusuf Ali. 2nd ed. 1977.

Howell, Alfred M. "Some notes on early treaties between Muslims and the Visigothic rulers of al-Andalus," in Actas del I Congreso de historia de Andalucía, diciembre, 1976. *Andalucía medieval,* vol. 1. Córdoba: 1978.

Indigenous Christian Communities in Medieval Islamic Lands: Conversion and Continuity. An International Conference in Medieval Studies. University of Toronto. October 23–25, 1986. (Publication of proceedings forthcoming.)

John, E. " 'Secularium Prioratus' and the Rule of St. Benedict," *Revue bénédictine* 75 (1965), pp. 212–39.

Jiménez Pedrajas, Raphael. "Las relaciones entre los cristianos y los musulmanes en Córdoba." *Boletín de la Real Academia de Córdoba de Ciencias, Bellas Letras y Nobles Artes* 80 (1960), pp. 107–236.

"San Eulogio de Córdoba, autor de la pasión francesa de los mártires mozárabes cordobeses Jorge, Aurelio y Natalia." *Anthologica Annua* 17 (1970), pp. 465–583.

Jones, Charles W. *Saints' Lives and Chronicles in Early Medieval England.* Ithaca, New York: 1947.

Kedar, Benjamin Z. *Crusade and Mission: European Attitudes toward the Muslims.* Princeton: 1984.

Khadduri, Majid. *War and Peace in the Law of Islam.* Baltimore: 1955.

Khoury, A. *Polemique byzantine contre l'Islam: VIIe au XIIIe siecles.* Leiden: 1972.

Lafuente y Zamalloa, Modesto. *Historia general de España.* 2nd ed. 15 vols. Madrid: 1869.

Lambert, Elie. "Le Voyage de saint Euloge dans les Pyrénées en 848." *Estudios dedicados a Menéndez Pidal,* 4:557–67. Madrid: 1953.

Langmuir, Gavin I. "Thomas of Monmouth: Detector of ritual murder." *Speculum* 59 (1984), pp. 820–46.

Lévi-Provençal, Evariste. *Histoire de l'Espagne musulmane.* 3 vols. 2nd ed. Paris: 1950.

Levtzion, Nehemiah, ed. *Conversion to Islam.* New York: 1979.

Lewis, Bernard. *The Jews of Islam.* Princeton: 1984.

Linage Conde, Emilio. *El Monacato en España e Hispanoamérica.* Salamanca: 1977.

MGH: *Monumenta Germaniae Historica.*

al-Makkari, Ahmed ibn Mohammed. *The History of the Mohammedan Dynasties in Spain.* Translated by Pascual de Gayangos. 2 vols. London: 1840.

Malone, E. E. "The monk and the martyr: the monk as the successor of the martyr." Dissertation, Catholic University of America, 1950.

Mariana, Juan de. *Historia general de España.* Madrid: 1789.

Meersseman, Gerard Gilles. "I Penitenti nei secoli XI e XII." *I laici nelle "societas christiana" dei secoli XI e XII.* Pubblicazione dell'Università Cattolica del Sacro Cuore. Miscellanea del Centro di Studi Medievali, 5. Milan: 1965.

Millares Carlo, Agustín. "Manuscritos visigóticos: notas bibliográficas." *Hispania Sacra* 14 (1961), pp. 337–444.

Millet-Gérard, Dominique. *Chrétiens mozarabes et culture islamique dans l'Espagne des VIIIᵉ–IXᵉ siècles.* Paris: 1984

Mones, Hussain. "Le rôle des hommes de religion dans l'histoire de l'Espagne musulmane jusqu'à la fin du califat." *Studia Islamica* 20 (1964).

Moorhead, John. "The earliest Christian theological response to Islam." *Religion* 11 (1981), 265–74.

Morales, Ambrosio de. *Corónica general de España.* . . . Edited by Benito Cano. 12 vols. Madrid: 1771–2.

Mortimer, R. C. *The Origins of Private Penance in the Western Church.* Oxford: 1939.

Moule, Charles F. D., ed. *Miracles; Cambridge Studies in their Philosophy and History.* London: 1965.

L'Occidente e l'Islam nell'alto medioevo: Settimane di studio del centro italiano di studi sull'alto medioevo XII. Spoleto: 1965.

Origen. *Contra Celsum.* Translated by Henry Chadwick. Cambridge: 1953.

Orlandis, José. *Estudios sobre instituciones monásticas medievales.* Pamplona: 1971.

PL: *Patrologiae cursus completus, series latina.* Edited by J. P. Migne et al.

Pelikan, Jaroslav. *The Growth of Medieval Theology: 600–1300.* Chicago: 1978.

Pérez de Urbel, Justo. *San Eulogio de Córdoba.* Madrid: 1927. Translation: *A Saint under Moslem Rule.* Translated by a Benedictine of Stanbrook Abbey. Milwaukee: 1937.

Richards, Jeffrey. *Consul of God: The Life and Times of Gregory the Great.* London: 1980.

Riddle, Donald. *The Martyrs, a Study in Social Control.* Chicago: 1931.

Rivera Recio, Juan Francisco. *Elipando de Toledo, nueva aportación a los estudios mozárabes.* Toledo: 1940.

Sage, Carleton M. "Paul Albar of Córdoba: Studies on his life and writings." Dissertation, Catholic University of America, 1943.

Sahas, D. J. *John of Damascus on Islam: the "Heresy of the Ishmaelites."* Leiden: 1972.

Samson. *Apologeticus.* CSM 2:506–658.

Severus. *History of the Patriarchs of the Coptic Church of Alexandria.* Edited by R. Graffin and F. Nau. Patrologia Orientalis. Vols. 1, 5, 6, 10. Paris: 1907–15.

Severus, Sulpicius. *Writings.* Translated by Bernard Peebles. Fathers of the Church, 7. Washington, D.C.: 1949.

Simonet Francisco X. *Historia de los mozárabes de España.* Madrid: 1903.

Smith, Morton. *Jesus the Magician.* New York: 1979.

Southern, Richard W. *Western Views of Islam in the Middle Ages.* Cambridge, Mass.: 1962.

Stancliffe, Clare. *St. Martin and his Biographer: History and Miracle in Sulpicius Severus.* Oxford: 1983.

Stillman, Norman A. *The Jews of Arab Lands.* Philadelphia: 1979.

Tentler, Thomas N. *Sin and Confession on the Eve of the Reformation.* Princeton: 1977.

Tritton, A. S. *The Caliphs and their Non-Muslim Subjects: A Critical Study of the Covenant of ʿUmar.* London: 1930.

Turki, Abdel Magid. "La vénération pour Mālik et la physionomie de malikisme andalou." *Studia Islamica* 33 (1971), pp. 41–65.

Turquet de Mayerne, Louis. *Histoire générale d'Espagne.* Translated by Edward Grimeston. London: 1612.

Urvoy, Dominique. "La pensée religieuse des mozarbes face à l'Islam." *Traditio* 39 (1983), pp. 419–32.

Van Dam, Raymond. "Hagiography and history: the life of Gregory Thaumaturgus." *Classical Antiquity* 1 (1982), pp. 272–308.

Vauchez, André. *La Sainteté en occident aux derniers siècles du moyen âge.* Rome: 1981.

Vives, José, ed. *Concilios visigóticos e hispano-romanos.* Barcelona: 1963.

Waltz, James. "The significance of the voluntary martyrs movement of ninth-century Córdoba." *Muslim World* 60 (1970), pp. 143–59, 226–36.

Wiegand, M. Gonsalva. "The Non-dramatic Works of Hrosvitha." Dissertation, St. Louis University, 1936.

Wolf, Kenneth Baxter. "The earliest Spanish Christian views of Islam." *Church History* 55 (1986), pp. 281–93.

Index